1993

University of St. Francis
GEN 813.52 M179
Madden, David

S0-BRP-434
3 0301 00088289 0

CAIN'S
CRAFT

by
David Madden

The Scarecrow Press, Inc.
Metuchen, N.J., & London   1985

LIBRARY
College of St. Francis
JOLIET, ILL.

<u>Frontispiece</u>:   Cain in 1934 publicity photo.

Library of Congress Cataloging in Publication Data

Madden, David, 1933-
    Cain's craft.

    Bibliography: p.
    Includes index.
    1. Cain, James M. (James Mallahan), 1892-1977--Criti-
cism and interpretation.   I. Title.
PS3505.A3113Z793 1985   813'.52   84-20215
ISBN 0-8108-1750-0

Copyright ©1985 by David Madden
Manufactured in the United States of America

813.52
m179

In Memory of

Harry T. Moore

147,896

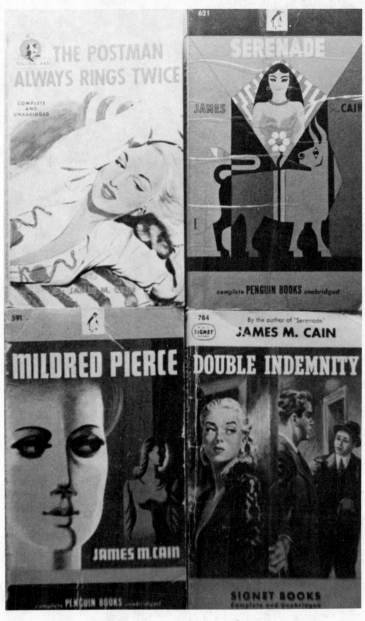

Photograph by Blake Madden.

CONTENTS

Acknowledgments   vii

Preface   ix

Chapter One   The Tough and Proletarian Novelists
                   of the Thirties: Cain's The Postman
                   Always Rings Twice, McCoy's They
                   Shoot Horses, Don't They?, and
                   Traven's The Death Ship   1

Chapter Two   Cain's Career as a Novelist   27

Chapter Three   Cain and the Movies of the Thirties
                   and Forties   37

Chapter Four   Cain and the "Pure" Novel   61

Chapter Five   A Comparison of Cain's The Postman
                   Always Rings Twice and Camus's The
                   Stranger   79

Chapter Six   The Aesthetics of Popular Culture:
                   Cain's Serenade and Morris's Love
                   Among the Cannibals: The Dynamics
                   of Craft and Technique   93

Bibliography   127

Index   149

James M. Cain in 1975, at age 82. Photograph by Roy
   Hoopes.

ACKNOWLEDGMENTS

James M. Cain offered cooperation in many ways and gave permission to quote from his published works and his letters. I am grateful to Alice Piper for permission to quote from Cain's works and private letters.

Material in this book originally appeared, in somewhat different form, in The University Review, The Journal of Popular Culture, Film Heritage, Papers on Language and Literature, and in James M. Cain, Twayne American Authors Series.

The distinctive insights of Peggy Bach, a reluctant Cain admirer, helped me in the revision and organization of the manuscript.

Given the current movie-generated revival of interest in James M. Cain, recently enhanced by the publication of the first full-scale biography, the question naturally arises, Is the book in hand an attempt, at least in part, to capitalize on that revival? I'm glad to be able to answer that Chapter Three of this study was written in the summer of 1960 in response to an intense nostalgia for movies made from Cain's novels in the forties, Double Indemnity, Mildred Pierce, and The Postman Always Rings Twice, when I was very young. I had always been aware of Cain as a writer, but had never gotten around to reading his novels. While studying playwriting with John Gassner at Yale Drama School, I went over to American Studies for a seminar with Norman Holmes Pearson. "Do a paper on a writer of your choice, sort of introducing his work to the reader," he told us. I was already in the middle of a book on Wright Morris that had grown out of a similar assignment in Leonard Wolf's graduate seminar at San Francisco State. Why I decided on Cain, I don't remember. Perhaps in reaction against the somewhat esoteric atmosphere of that Yale seminar.

I read most of Cain's novels and stories, wrote to Cain himself; my writing about Cain and to Cain continued up to his death in 1977. Pearson liked the paper, The University Review in Kansas (now New Letters) published it in 1963, and Twayne published my book-length study in 1970. So my critical studies of Morris, which got started in 1957, and of Cain were pursued parallel for over twenty years, while I was writing criticism of other writers and my own fiction as well. Most of the material in this book appeared first as separate essays that were intended all along as parts of the Twayne study. Only the last chapter was written later; it consists of two different essays that appeared in Journal of Popular Culture, in the last part of which my continuing interests in Cain and Morris converge.

Perhaps it was my immersion in Morris' aesthetics that made me turn as a kind of relief to the clear-cut craft of Cain's fiction. My study of Cain led me to other tough-guy writers and to proletarian writers; the two apparently divergent types intersect in violence. Tough Guy Writers of the Thirties and Proletarian Writers of the Thirties appeared simultaneously in 1968, two years before the Cain book came out. Meanwhile, the concept of the American Dream that I saw at the heart of Morris' work, making me aware of its very different development in Cain, resulted in American Dreams, American Nightmares, a collection of essays scrutinizing that compelling image in the works of several major American novelists, playwrights, and poets. A revival of interest in Nathanael West caused many of the critics I had asked to contribute original essays to American Dreams to produce more good pieces on West than I could include. Nathanael West: The Cheaters and the Cheated (1973) was my solution to that happy dilemma.

I have woven this tapestry to suggest why I want to approach the works of Cain once again. I have rejected the alternative of updating and reprinting James M. Cain. Twayne did not publicize the books in its series; the publication of a book on Cain coming out in 1970 needed some kind of attention. By 1977, it was out of print; its sale of about 1,500 copies did not truly reflect the interest in Cain, especially if one considers the steady, strong interest in Tough Guy Writers of the Thirties, in which Cain is a central figure. What I want this book to do then, is to demonstrate my interest in Cain as it developed through various related interests from 1960 to 1984.

The first chapter poses the question, What is the significance of Cain's fiction in the context of the tough guy and the related proletarian fiction of the thirties? One way to focus an answer to that question is to compare his most characteristic and perhaps most successful novel The Postman Always Rings Twice with another "pure" tough-guy novel, They Shoot Horses, Don't They? by Horace McCoy, and with a tough-guy proletarian novel, The Death Ship by B. Traven.

To Cain, from his early days as a journalist to the end of his life, writing was a good way to make a living, it was a career. In the second chapter, I trace Cain's career as a popular novelist making a living by working at his craft.

Another facet of Cain's career as a writer is his attempt to write screenplays in Hollywood, a floundering career from the start, one that preceded his career as a novelist and that affected his fictional techniques. To show the influence of his novels upon other fiction writers and upon movies through a circuitous route, I discuss in Chapter Three the critical reception of movies made from his novels over the years, up to the present.

Cain's characters, their predicaments, the subject matter and themes of his fiction are so simple, the reader responds directly to the craft itself (style, pace, dialog, etc.); his most effective fiction approaches the "pure" novel. Chapter Four is an overview of his novels through the perspective of the concept of the "pure" novel.

An answer to the question of Cain's influence upon European fiction is suggested in a detailed comparison of The Postman Always Rings Twice with Camus's The Stranger, which is also, of course, a very different novel that provides a contrast to a study of Cain's craft and of other typical elements in his fiction.

The case of Cain's entire career as journalist, scriptwriter, and novelist contributes to the effort to understand the workings of popular culture. My emphasis on Cain's craft leads to the larger question, Can a meaningful and useful aesthetics of popular culture be developed? One way to focus an answer to that question is to compare Cain's craft in Serenade (1937) with the subtler techniques of Wright Morris, who is in no way influenced by Cain, in a similar novel written two decades later, Love Among the Cannibals.

I have restructured, revised, and updated these essays and organized them to show Cain in six different perspectives: the tough and proletarian writers; popular fiction writing as a career; writing for the movies and the adaptation of novels to the movies; the pure novel; the influence of American fiction on European fiction; the aesthetics of popular culture, the comparison of the craft of a "popular" novel with the techniques of a "serious" novel. Each of those perspectives is of interest, I assume, in itself.

To facilitate ease of reading, I have worked all references into the text, using brief forms of citation; full bibliographical information appears in the annotated bibliography.

David Madden
Baton Rouge

The Tough and Proletarian
Novelists of the Thirties:
Cain's The Postman Always
Rings Twice, McCoy's They
Shoot Horses, Don't They?,
and Traven's The Death Ship

Three related genres that developed in the novel form
during the thirties were the hard-boiled private detective
(which departed from the genteel English novel of detection),
the proletarian (which derived from European naturalism and
American selective realism), and the tough guy (which derived from the former two). But perhaps for the best and
most influential work of all three genres "the tough-guy
novel" is a good term: Dashiell Hammett's The Maltese
Falcon (1929) and Raymond Chandler's The Big Sleep (1939),
in the private detective realm; B. Traven's The Death Ship
(1926; American edition, 1934), among proletarian novels;
and Horace McCoy's They Shoot Horses, Don't They? (1935),
among the pure tough-guy books, are all minor classics in
American literature. The twenty-minute egg of the hard-
boiled school is James M. Cain; and the quintessential tough-
guy novel is The Postman Always Rings Twice (1934).

All these novels--and indeed most of the hard-boiled
and pure tough novels, as well as some of the best proletarian works--were published by Knopf, with the exception
of McCoy's, although I Should Have Stayed Home (1938) was.
Blanche Knopf was Hammett's, Cain's, and Chandler's editor.
A house conception grouped the big three best-selling authors, as when the cover of Publishers Weekly reminded
booksellers that in 1929 there was Hammett, in 1934 Cain,
and alerted them to the appearance in 1939 of Chandler.
Neither Traven nor McCoy sold well in the United States;
much of Traven's work was published first in Germany, and
one McCoy novel appeared first in England; Traven has long

had a permanent, estimable international reputation; McCoy was valued highly in France in the forties.

One of the first critics of eminence to discuss Cain seriously was Edmund Wilson. In 1940, he introduced the readers of The New Republic to "The Boys in the Back Room": James M. Cain and John O'Hara (later, he added John Steinbeck, Horace McCoy, William Saroyan, Hans Otto Storm, Nathanael West, and a few others). In this famous essay, Wilson called them "poets of the tabloid murder," a phrase which has echoed down the decades. All these writers had lived in and written about California. "They thus constitute a sort of group to which we might add Hammett, Chandler, and Traven, and they suggest certain generalizations" (19). These generalizations go much further than Wilson took them. There are remarkably detailed similarities in the life and work of these writers that can't be gone into here either.

The significance of the tough-guy novel as exemplified in the works of Cain, these other, and similar writers extends beyond pure entertainment into basic aesthetic and social values. The tough-guy novel reflected the hard surfaces, inadvertently expressed the mood, and provided an impersonal vision of American civilization during the Depression. It stimulated the action element in motion pictures. It affected the tone and attitude of more "serious" writers. And inspired some European novelists during the forties.

In its special way, the tough-guy vision scrutinizes one of the central themes in American literature: the fate of American land, character, and dream. (Dream-seeker Gatsby, appropriately enough, rose from the underworld.) Leaving out the subtle phases between, the tough novelists show the failure of the dream by a camera-cold recording of the nightmare. Without attempting psychological analysis, they create psychological myths. Popular fiction can tell us much about ordinary people in a way that "serious" fiction, because it is aimed at an intellectual, aesthetically inclined minority, cannot. And tough novels are social documents, verifiable not by statistics but by facts of human nature as expressed at a certain time in a way appropriate to the social and cultural climate of that time. With a purity of vision unimpaired by ideology, the tough novel projects a "surface picture of American violence" in the thirties. Violence is always close to the surface in a civilization resolutely committed to goals which create conditions for it as a kind of by-product.

Generally, scholars of American literature give Cain and the tough-guy writers merely a passing glance; like travelers who must pass through the slum outskirts to reach the heart of a great city, they are a little fascinated, a little repelled and certainly relieved to have passed through. But they see immediately the tough novel's literary line of descent: the European naturalism of Zola, the Americanized naturalism of Frank Norris and Dreiser, commingled with the European realism of Flaubert and Balzac, the American selective realism of Stephen Crane. Frederick Hoffman sums up the impact of naturalism in The Modern Novel in America, citing the tough novel as its latest manifestation. "The influence of Dreiser, Farrell, and Hemingway is pervasive. Beyond that, the slickness of John O'Hara's conceptions has been added to the contribution made by James Cain to the surface picture of American violence" (205).

A distinction must be made between the traditional novel of detection (Poe, A. A. Milne, Freeman Will Crofts, Dorothy Sayers, Agatha Christie) and the hard-boiled mystery novel (Hammett, Chandler, Lester Dent, Frank Gruber, George Coxe, Raoul Whitfield, Richard Sale). Developed by Poe to full fruition in only four stories, the detective story was our first literary export. Attracted and repulsed by the American taste for violence, the English adopted--even before Poe could be imitated in America--and domesticated the form. W. H. Auden testified that one becomes addicted, as to tobacco or alcohol. Discriminating writers and critics read detective novels: André Gide, Robert Graves, André Malraux, T. S. Eliot, Paul Elmer More, Jacques Barzun, Somerset Maugham, Bernard De Voto, Joseph Wood Krutch; some even wrote "esoteric" defenses of the form; G. K. Chesterton wrote detective stories. In a time when fiction was dominated by philosophical, psychological, and symbolic concerns, the detective story offered simple storytelling and a pure, though crude, aesthetic pleasure. William Aydelotte suggests that because the complex problems of modern existence have been banished from the secure universe of unrealistic conventions, life is not more horrible, but more cheerful, and events are endowed with a garish significance and glamor. With the discovery of the murderer, we are gratified by the illusion of being released from guilt, disassociated from the killer, who acts as communal scapegoat ("The Detective Story as Historical Source," 76-95).

The genteel English novel of detection prevailed until the thirties. Then, with the publication of Hammett's Red

<u>Harvest</u> (1929), hard-boiled detective fiction stepped out of the
pulp pages of <u>Black Mask</u> and into hardcover respectability,
thus contributing to the decline and fall of the traditional
whodunit. Slightly adapted, what critics said about Hammett
is descriptive of Cain and of the tough-guy novel in general
as well. In <u>Murder for Pleasure</u>, Howard Haycraft delineated
Hammett's contribution: "Hammett's lean, dynamic, un-
sentimental narratives created a definitely <u>American style</u>,
quite separate and distinct from the accepted English pattern."
His are "penetrating if often shocking novels of manners" and
of character. "Yet they are as sharply stylized and deliberately artificial as Restoration Comedy, and have been called
an inverted form of romanticism ... commercial in inception
... and they miss being Literature, if at all, by the narrow-
est margins" (169-171). In <u>The Simple Art of Murder</u>
(1952), Chandler offered a practitioner's point of view.
"Hammett took murder out of the Venetian vase" of the
English drawing room "and dropped it into the alley."

   Hammett wrote at first (and almost to the end) for

> people with a sharp, aggressive attitude to life.
> They were not afraid of the seamy side of things;
> they lived there. Violence did not dismay them;
> it was right down their street. Hammett gave mur-
> der back to the kind of people that commit it for
> reasons, not just to provide a corpse; and with the
> means at hand, not hand-wrought dueling pistols....
> He put these people down on paper as they were,
> and he made them talk and think in the language they
> customarily used for these purposes (190).

W. H. Auden testified that Chandler himself was "interested
in writing, not detective stories, but serious studies of a
criminal milieu, the Great Wrong Place, and his powerful
but extremely depressing books should be read and judged,
not as escape literature, but as works of art" ("The Guilty
Vicarage," 190).

   Hammett and Chandler directly aroused the fears and
nightmare images of American civilization in the thirties.
In "A Cosmic View of the Private Eye," John Paterson observed that the novel of detection presented the kind of world
we like to <u>think</u> we live in, but the private eye introduces
disorder, because he represents the world we <u>really</u> live in,
one which offers no closed solution; he is an exile, estranged

from all community structure, as each of us is in his private
self. "He speaks for men who have lost faith in the values
of their society" (The Saturday Review, 7-8, 31-33). Though
their purpose was not deliberately to depict the social evils of
the time, Hammett's and Chandler's good-bad guy private
detectives were guides who conducted Americans on a tour
of the underworld, into its alleys and down its "mean streets."
Hypocrisy in religion, deceit and self-interest in business, and
corruption in politics seeped down into these alleys and created
"messes" that Sam Spade and Philip Marlowe had to clean up.
Seeing life with the impartiality of the camera eye, they soft-
ened their hard-boiled attitude with neither sentiment nor moral
judgment. "The private eye is not the dandy turned sleuth,"
says Leslie Fiedler, "he is the cowboy adapted to life on the
city streets, the embodiment of innocence moving untouched
through universal guilt ... the blameless shamus is also the
honest proletarian, illuminating by contrast the decadent society of the rich.... " (Love and Death in the American
Novel, 75).

What was the special appeal of the private eye novels
of Hammett and Chandler, as opposed to the cool puzzle
appeal of the novel of detection? Chandler's explanation accounts in part for the appeal of Cain's pure tough novels as
well: it wasn't violence, fine writing, originality of plot or
character.

> Possibly it was the smell of fear which these stories
> managed to generate. Their characters lived in a
> world gone wrong, a world in which, long before the
> atom bomb, civilization had created the machinery
> for its own destruction, and was learning to use it
> with all the moronic delight of a gangster trying out
> his first machine gun. The law was something to be
> manipulated for profit and power. The streets were
> dark with something more than night. The mystery
> story grew hard and cynical about motive and charac-
> ter, but it was not cynical about the effects it tried
> to produce nor about its technique of producing them.

A few unusual critics with "very open" minds recognized this
(Simple Art, vii). "The story of our time to me is not war,
not atomic energy but the marriage of an idealist to a gangster
and how their home life and children turned out" (Twentieth
Century Authors, First Supplement, 186-87). To write about
the world we actually live in, it took "writers with tough minds
and a cool spirit of detachment ... down these mean streets
a man must go who is not himself mean, who is neither tar-

nished nor afraid," said Chandler, speaking now of the hero
(Simple Art, 193).

    If the hard-boiled technique in the mystery was intro-
duced by Hammett and developed by Chandler, it degenerated,
according to Ben Ray Redman's analysis, with Mickey Spillane.
Mike Hammer is a caricature of Marlowe, a rampant expression
of fascist and sadist tendencies in the American concept of
masculinity. Redman laments of the fact that crime has replaced detection, that barbarians have replaced the old detectives. Full of exhibitionism, sadism, sexual intercourse,
homosexuality, and flagellation, the detective novel in 1952
was improbable, incredible, and absurd ("Decline and Fall
of the Whodunit," 8, 31).

    Chandler wanted a clear distinction made between his
own kind of novel and Cain's. Frank MacShane, Chandler's
biographer, quotes a letter Chandler wrote his publisher,
Knopf in 1943.

> I hope that day will come when I don't have to ride
> around on Hammett and James Cain.... Hammett
> is all right ... But James Cain--faugh! Every-
> thing he touches smells like a billygoat. He is
> every kind of writer I detest, a faux naïf, a Proust
> in greasy overalls, a dirty little boy with a piece of
> chalk and a board fence and nobody looking. Such
> people are the offal of literature, not because they
> write about dirty things, but because they do it in a
> dirty way. Nothing hard and clean and cold and
> ventilated. A brothel with a smell of cheap scent
> in the front parlor and a bucket of slops at the back
> door. Do I, for God's sake, sound like that?

"The dislike of Cain," says MacShane, "goes deeper, for it
reflects Chandler's romantic, even sentimental, view of the
world...."

> Chandler's distaste for Cain's prose is an aspect
> of his dislike of his moral position. Chandler ex-
> aggerates ... for there are moments of lyricism
> in The Postman Always Rings Twice and in Serenade
> ... what is missing is the tension that exists when
> people have some possibility of choice. It there-
> fore lacks the poetry that distinguished Chandler's
> prose.

But Chandler's excellent poetry was laminated onto his prose;
Cain's was evoked by a lean prose that <u>seemed</u> lacking in
poetry (<u>The Life of Raymond Chandler</u>, 100).

In Hemingway, Hammett, and Chandler the raw masculine power to kill became a mystique, but few of Cain's
characters use a gun, though Cain is always associated with
"the false power of the gun." Cain has never written a detective story--not even in the Hammett-Chandler vein.
<u>Double Indemnity</u> and <u>The Embezzler</u> have been cited as
borderline novels; the little-known, low-quality <u>Sinful Woman</u>
and <u>Jealous Woman</u> are even closer to the type. But Cain's
stories are concerned with murder and love, from the criminal's point of view, exclusively, though he may begin as an
insurance investigator. Cain is more interested in making
action suggest an explanation of the crime as it is being per-
petrated than in constructing a solution out of the swamps of
mystification. In several novels, he even departs from the
pure tough-guy type, as in <u>Career in C Major</u> and <u>Mildred
Pierce</u>.

Just as one must distinguish between the formal detective story begun by Poe and the private-eye thrillers begun by
Hammett, one must also distinguish between the thriller and
the "pure" tough-guy novel, though they developed concurrently
and cross-fertilized each other. Neither Cain nor McCoy
exemplify in their characteristic works either the formal or
the thriller-detective type. A product of all the forces referred to in this study, the pure tough novel nevertheless is
a separate type which presents a hard-boiled picture of life
for its own sake, without the justification of either an ideology or a conventional form, whether strictly adhered to or
consciously violated.

This tough vision of life is cynical or pessimistic; the
attitude is ironic, dispassionate, neutral; the tone is hard-
boiled, having no cultural pretensions, expressing no tender
emotions. The first person point of view is used, almost
exclusively; the syntax, diction, and grammar are those of
the characters; the imagery is stark, rarely lyrical. The
characters are vivid, elemental, somewhat two-dimensional.
The setting, environment, atmosphere is that of the large
cities, with a special recurrence of Southern California as
the locale. The scene method is dominant, with a predomi-
nance of blunt, brisk dialogue. The action is swiftly paced.
The technical control, given the simplicity and skeletonal
elements is absolute. The impact of these novels derives
from their brevity; their average length is 190 pages.

The tough attitude had so pervaded all forms of mass entertainment and literature that Saul Bellow's hero opened his 1944 novel, The Dangling Man, with this observation:

> ... this is an era of hardboiled-dom. Today, the
> code of the athlete, of the tough boy--an American
> inheritance, I believe, from the English gentleman
> --that curious mixture of striving, asceticism, and
> rigor, the origins of which some trace back to
> Alexander the Great--is stronger than ever. Do
> you have feelings? There are correct and incorrect
> ways of indicating them. Do you have an inner
> life? It is nobody's business but your own. Do
> you have emotions? Strangle them. To a degree,
> everybody obeys this code. And it does admit of
> a limited kind of candor, a closemouthed straight-
> forwardness. But on the truest candor, it has an
> inhibitory effect. Most serious matters are closed
> to the hard-boiled. They are unpracticed in intro-
> spection and therefore badly equipped to deal with
> opponents whom they cannot shoot like big game or
> outdo in daring (7).

James T. Farrell stresses the fact that in his back-ground Cain is intimately associated with the twenties of Mencken, observing that in the early forties his writing still suggested the sophistication of The Mercury. But while Mencken encouraged a more serious exploration of American experience in fiction, and created an audience for it, Cain, Farrell charges, failed to grow with the positive side of Mencken's approach. "I think it not unfair to say that writing like Cain's exploits rather than explores the material of life in America" ("Cain's Movietone Realism," 85). Critics like Farrell accuse Cain of presenting violence without context, sadism without motive, death without dignity, sex without love, money with-out comfort, murder without malice, as though these things were not to be observed everywhere around Cain; and yet they lament his failure to make his work socially significant. It is not enough for Farrell, and others, that Cain provides images, typical characters, situations, of the times in which he writes, it is not enough that the novels themselves are characteristic artifacts of the times--Cain must render, like Farrell, some judgment on what he depicts. Farrell allows that in Cain exists "the taste for reality" which he acquired in the twenties. "But to it he has added lessons learned from Hollywood. Cain now shocks with his calculated thrills the yokels he attacked in Our Government" (1930).

Cain once suggested that the yokels got what they deserved.
"These same yokels deserve the realist they now have and
that realist deserves his audience" (86).   It is an audience,
Cain has often remarked, of which he strives to be worthy.
Ironically, Farrell's and Cain's novels were often reviewed
or discussed together; Stanley Edgar Hyman, Dawn Powell,
W. M. Frohock, and others observed that though Farrell was
more "important" and "serious, " Cain was more successful
in holding his reader.

        Cain, then, is preeminently a man of the twenties
and thirties whose fiction somehow evokes a sense of the
early forties as well, but who has little to say, directly
or indirectly, to the fifties and sixties in the novels of those
decades. His early works continue to be relevant, while his
new ones do little to expand his contribution to the tough-guy
vision of American land, character, and dream.

                                    2.

        A comparison of Cain's most effective novel, The
Postman Always Rings Twice, with Horace McCoy's They
Shoot Horses, Don't They? and with B. Traven's The Death
Ship may provide a perspective for seeing the similarities
and differences of tough-guy and proletarian fiction, for dis-
tinguishing those two types from novels of detection, from
private-eye crime novels, such as Hammett's and Chandler's,
and for examining characteristics of Cain's distinctive novels
more clearly. McCoy's novels come closest to Cain's;
Traven's novels are quite different from either Cain's or
McCoy's.

        Although Frank Chambers, the twenty-four-year-old
narrator of The Postman Always Rings Twice (1934), belongs
to the lumpenproletariat, to that legion of unemployed who
became tramps of the road, hoboes of the rails, and migrant
workers, Cain is not deliberately interested in depicting the
social ills of his times. His manner of dramatizing facets
of American experience provides insights (expressionistically
exaggerated perhaps) into the American dream turned nightmare, the all-American boy turned tough guy. If there is
an attack on conditions that produced a man like Frank, it
is only implicit. Frank is an easygoing fellow, remarkably
free of bitterness, even when given cause; although he commits
murder and pistol-whips a blackmailer, he is not willfully

vicious. A spontaneous creature of action whose psychological nature readily accommodates ambivalent attitudes, he can
be fond of Nick Papadakis, yet seduce his young wife Cora,
and attempt to kill him twice, then weep at his funeral.

And although this novel is concerned, as many of Cain's
are, with murder and other forms of violence, and although
it satisfied momentarily the average American's inexhaustible
craving for details of crime and punishment, it cannot be
classified as a detective tale. Cain, like the readers he
has in mind, is fascinated by the intricacies of the law and
of insurance claims, but his primary interest is in presenting
an inside view of the criminal act. However, Frank is no
gangster and Cora is no moll; they are not far removed in
status or aspiration from the average anticipated reader of
Cain.

For Frank and Cora lie down in the great American
dreambed of the twenties, only to wake up in a living nightmare in the thirties. A lurid decade produced such a lurid
tale. When they meet at Nick's Twin Oaks Tavern on a
highway outside Los Angeles, Frank has just been thrown off
a truck, having sneaked into the back for a ride up from
Tijuana, and Cora is washing dishes in the restaurant. To
demonstrate the animal impact of their encounter, Cain has
them meet on page 5, make love on page 15, and plot to
murder her obese, middle-aged Greek husband on page 23.
In the typical Cain novel, a man and a woman set out on a
dangerous adventure. The object? For the man: the woman.
For the woman: money. And murder is inevitable. Sharing
the dream of getting drunk and making love without hiding,
they go on what Cain calls "the Love-Rack." "The wish
that comes true," says Cain, is a terrifying thing. The screws
tighten on the love rack as soon as Frank and Cora believe
that they have gotten, away with murder and have acquired
money, property, and freedom.

But in the background each has another dream which
mocks the shared realization of the immediate wish. Cora
came to Hollywood from a small town in Iowa bemused by
the dream most girls of the thirties cherished: to become a
movie star. She failed, and Nick rescued her from a hash
house. But basically her values are middle-class, and above
all she wants respectability, even if murder is the prerequi-
site. An anachronism in the age of technology, though he
has a certain skill as a garage mechanic, Frank desires
to be always on the move, compelled by something of the

spirit of the open road that Whitman celebrated. For a moment, but only for a moment, he shares this romantic, idyl-
lic vision with Cora. After the failure of their first attempt
to murder Nick, they set out together for a life of wandering.
Thus, in the criminal affair of these lovers, these deliberate
outsiders, two central dreams of the American experience--
unrestrained mobility and respectable sedentariness--and two
views of the American landscape--the open road and the mortgaged house--collide. As the dreams finally betray them,
they begin, ironically, to turn on each other, for basically
what Frank wants is Cora, the sexual dynamo, and what Cora
wants is an instrument to be used to gain her ends--money
and respectability. Though she may convince herself that the
right man, instead of a fat foreigner, is a necessary part of
her aspirations, this man would soon wake up in the wrong
dream.

    While the novel's larger thematic dimensions exist in
the background, as a kind of fable of the American experience, giving it a lasting value in our literature, Cain is
more immediately concerned with the lovers and the action
that results from their wish. This action keeps in motion
certain elements that almost guarantee the reader's interest:
illicit love; murder; the smell of tainted money; sexual violence that verges on the abnormal; and the strong character-
izations of such men as Sackett, the district attorney; Katz,
the eccentric lawyer; and Madge, the pick-up who takes Frank
to South America to capture pumas. Cain plays upon the
universal wishes of the average American male.

    What fascinates serious readers of literature is Cain's
technique for manipulating reader response. Not only does
he almost automatically achieve certain thematic ironies inherent in his raw material, but the ironies of action are
stunningly executed. For instance, Frank cons Nick out of a
free meal, but the con backfires in a way when Nick cons
Frank into staying on to operate the service station; thus
Frank becomes involved in a situation that will leave three
people dead. After recovering from what he took to be an
accident in the bathtub, Nick searches for Frank and persuades him to return to the roadside restaurant, thus help-
ing to bring about his own death. Cleared of killing the
Greek, Frank and Cora collect the insurance. Later, when
she is waiting for a taxi to leave Frank, Cora sticks a note
for him in the cash register; it refers to their having killed
the Greek for his money. But Frank catches her and insists
that he loves her; to test his love, Cora, who is now pregnant,

swims so far out to sea that Frank will have to help her
back; he does help her, but driving back from the beach,
they have a wreck and she is killed.   The police find the
note in the cash register and conclude that Frank has engi-
neered the wreck so that he can have all the money.   Because he cannot be tried twice for killing the Greek, they
execute him for murdering Cora.   A careful pattern of minor
ironies contributes to the impact of the major ones.

Cain's structural techniques are impressive.   The
swift execution of the basic situation in the first twenty-three
pages has been noted, and each development, each scene, is
controlled with the same narrative skill; inherent in each episode is the inevitability of the next.   Everything is kept
strictly to the essentials; the characters, for instance, exist
only for the immediate action; there is almost no exposition
as such.   Cain is the acknowledged master of pace.   Violence
and sexual passion are thrust forward at a rate that is itself
part of the reader's vicarious experience.   Contributing to
this sense of pace is the swift rhythm of the dialogue, which
also manages to keep certain undercurrents flowing.   Frank's
character justified the economy of style, the nerve-end ad-
herence to the spine of the action.

As a force in the tough school, Cain contributed to
the revolutionary restructuring of much of European fiction in
the thirties and forties.   American literature first made a
strong impact on the world through the tough novel;   European literary historians stress this phenomenon.   Objective
and dispassionate, the tough writers dispensed with the
Jamesean analysis of the psychological inner life and made
character delineation subordinate to expressive action.   Deeply pessimistic, they denied the validity of established insti-
tutions and attitudes by showing the futility of the wish come
true, and by refusing to judge violent behavior in an absurd
world.   Cain was received on a level with Hemingway and
Faulkner.   Americans were too steeped in tough-fiction to see
The Postman's originality as the French did.

3.

In the pure tough-guy genre, a better book than The
Postman (and perhaps than The Stranger), for a projection
of the existential predicament through a kind of allegory, is
Horace McCoy's They Shoot Horses, Don't They? originally
published by Simon & Schuster in 1935.   Though well
reviewed, the hardcover edition made little public impact; the

1948 paperback, however, was a Signet Edition bestseller;
Avon reissued it in 1966 and again in 1969 when the movie
appeared.   It has a natural symbolism in Pound's sense of
the term: the natural object is the most effective symbol.
McCoy has much of Cain's talent for economy and pace, but
he consciously illustrates man's condition in the Depression
through the single metaphor of the marathon dance, upon
which he focuses more resolutely than Cain and Camus do
upon their central actions; and he is less overtly philosophical than Camus, relying solely upon the deliberate mechanics of his metaphor.   This novel thus stands between Cain
and Camus and is as close a combination of the pure novel
and the philosophical as exists in the "tough" school.

Thomas Sturak objects to Wilson's laying the mark of
Cain on McCoy, denying that They Shoot Horses, Don't They?
was one of those books "which apparently derived" from
Cain's sensational first novel.   As Kiss Tomorrow Goodbye
was going into production, McCoy urged Random House to
disassociate his work from "the 'James Cain' school."   He
often had occasion to resent the "almost obligatory" comparison to Cain's Postman.   In 1948, he wrote Signet, "I do not
care for Cain's work, although there may be much he can
teach me.   I know this though--continued labeling of me as
of 'the Cain school' (whatever the hell that is) and I shall
slit either his throat or mine" (146).   Nothing tough about
McCoy.   His latent reformist tendencies are clear enough in
No Pockets in a Shroud (1937; American edition, paper 1948),
but he was never a proletarian writer.   One English critic,
having declared that it was "emphatically not just another
example of that fake American, romantic tough writing,"
asserted that They Shoot Horses, Don't They? implied "a
condemnation of American civilization severe enough to satisfy the standard of the Third International" ("Horace McCoy's
Objective Lyricism," 148).

Robert, the young narrator who aspires to become a
film director like Eisenstein, is not a bum.   His tough tone
simply reflects the effect a brutalizing experience has had
upon him.   An unemployed movie extra in the middle of the
Depression, Robert meets Gloria, a not very attractive, unemployed extra who persuades him to enter a marathon dance
contest as her partner.   Both have come to Hollywood, glamor
capital of the world, from small Southern towns, lured by the
American dream of sudden success.   After an unsuccessfull
suicide attempt before she left home, Gloria is now being
"razzed" by an expert--God;   but she lacks the courage

to kill herself. Her verbal signature throughout the contest is some variation on the refrain, "I wish I was dead." Opposed to this total despair is Robert's typical American optimism; but he ends a victim of Gloria's nihilistic vision. Like Cain's Frank Chambers and Camus' Meursault, Robert and Gloria exist only in terms of their situation as contestants; they have almost no past, and their future is violent death.

The contest is held on an amusement pier in an old building that was once a public dance hall. One hundred and forty couples enter: professional marathon dancers and amateurs, like Robert and Gloria. Floor judges, nurses, and a house doctor are in attendance; contestants are allowed to continue only if they are in good physical condition. The dancing area is thirty by one hundred feet; there are loge, circus, or general admission seats, and a bar. Contestants dance one hour and fifty minutes; during the ten-minute rest intervals, they sleep, eat, shave, bathe, excrete, change clothes. The trick is to learn to do several things at once. After the first week, contestants need not dance, they must simply keep moving; all employees of the hall must constantly be in motion. Local sponsors of individual couples provide equipment and costumes, the company name across the chest, the contestant's number on his back. Thus, Robert and Gloria become "Jonathan Beer." Specialty numbers draw a shower of silver; but one couple, who do a lifeless tap dance, declare that you are better off without a specialty. In the derby, a nightly fifteen-minute heel-and-toe endurance race, ("one good way to kill us off," says Gloria) Robert stops trying to win and strives merely to keep from coming in last, to avoid being disqualified. "All the weaklings had been eliminated" (104). If a dancer loses his partner, because of menstrual pains or a heart attack, for instance, he may couple with another lone survivor; casualties are scarcely missed. A tub of ice water awaits those who faint; thus is Robert shocked out of a dream of being a film director. The main inducement for staying in the contest is that one knows where his next meal is coming from; food and bed are free as long as the contestant endures. For the winning couple the purse is one thousand dollars, and every one has the same chance, according to Rocky Gravo, the master of ceremonies. There is also the chance of being "discovered" by a movie producer, though after the second day each contestant resembles a zombie. It is a contest of "endurance and skill"; one must have the skill to endure.

Gloria's attitude is overwhelmingly cynical. The TLS
reviewer characterized Gloria as "the embodiment of the out-
cast, unemployed and unemployable, miserable, cynical,
foul-mouthed, without faith in anything or anybody, very nearly worthless," but "to some small extent redeemed by honesty
and pitiless self-knowledge" (in Sturak, 154). Gloria says,
"I know where I stand" (125). She and Robert are on a
merry-go-round; when the dance is over, they will get off
where they got on. Eating and sleeping is merely a postpon-
ing of death. Responding to Robert's expression of sympathy
for one of the dancers who is arrested as a fugitive murderer,
Gloria suggests that they are all condemned fugitives. "Socks,"
the promoter, appreciates the publicity; anything that draws
the crowds is good. He asks Gloria and Robert to get married on the dance floor as a "high class" entertainment feature; they can get a divorce after the contest closes. "It's
just a show business angle," says Socks. Gloria refuses;
Robert is afraid the angry promoter will disqualify them.
Gloria, who wishes she had never been born, encourages one
of the dancers who is pregnant to abort the child because it
will only end up in the same way.

In the twenties and the thirties, dance marathons, an
import from Europe, were held in every major American
city. Sturak quotes McCoy: "there were decadence and evil
in the old walkathons--and violence. The evil, of course,
as evil always has and always will, fascinated the customer
and the violence possesses a peculiar lyricism that elevated
the thing into the realm of high art" (142). Hollywood is a particularly apt symbolic setting for McCoy's marathon; it represents the public Eden to which few are admitted; the rejects
end up on the dance floor. The roll call of actual celebrities
among the spectators is effective, more so today since we
can see what fame comes to. In the context of the Depression, the spectators are the corrupt rich being amused by the
antics of the work horses, but ultimately spectator and dancer
reverse roles. Just as the dance, symbol of the new postwar
morality, became perverted by the marathon, sexual perver-
sion is part of the experience. Gloria is about to submit to
lesbians to get what she wants; Mrs. Layden, a wealthy old
woman who comes every night to watch, lusts for Robert.
Robert and Gloria are not in love; there is not even a sexual
tie. About to do a favor for a nymphomaniac dancer under
the bandstand, Robert is interrupted by a voice in the dark;
later, he learns that Gloria was nearby with Rocky. Rocky's
monontonous exhortation to the orchestra, the dancers (especially the females), and the audience is "Give!"

When a rich spectator finally shows an interest in
her, Gloria, ironically, is too devoid of hope to respond.
She declares that she is glad she is through with life.   In
the midst of a fight in the bar, the cause of which is never
disclosed, five shots are fired.   Mrs. Layden, on her way
to the platform to judge the derby, is an accidental target.
Ironically, old Mrs. Layden wanted to live to make love to
young Robert, while Gloria wishes the bullet had struck herself.   Without a winner, the marathon ends on the dictate of
chance.   Robert and Gloria walk out onto the pier.   She persuades him that she is no good to herself nor to anyone else,
that she is better off dead.   He shoots her to put her out of
her misery.   Ironically, his lawyer instructs Robert to throw
himself on the mercy of the court; but the court gives him,
against his will, what he gave Gloria at her own request--
oblivion.

While the marathon dance symbolizes man's predicament in the thirties, it is almost perfect as a symbolic expression of the universal human predicament.   It is what
Chandler called "pure art."   Technically, says Sturak, They
Shoot Horses, Don't They? "is a brilliant tour de force"
(150).   "The deep strain of 'symbolism'" in the novel, "not
the hard-boiled surface--is its dominant aesthetic characteristic" (161).

> ...   the atmospheric intensity and inevitable fatal-
> ity of They Shoot Horses, Don't They? speak ...
> convincingly for McCoy's artistry....   With bold
> originality and high degree of literary skill, he
> imbued his story with the bitter and disquieted mood
> from which he wrote, creating one of the most orig-
> inal works of contemporary American fiction....
> McCoy's marathon dance macabre has become a
> universally applicable parable of modern man's ex-
> istential predicament" (162).

While McCoy's central symbolic action is realistically true
and stark, and never literary, the dance draws to itself many
traditional connotations that enhance the significance of the
marathon.   In mythic terms, the grinding dance is like Sisyphus' struggle to push his rock to the top of the mountain;
the ten-minute rest periods are like his moments of freedom
as he returns to his burden on the plain.   In the simple
event of the dance, we experience a pure existential situation
that exemplifies the absurd nature of life.

Among the most effective motifs, all of which McCoy
develops quite naturally, is the incessant pounding of the
ocean under the floor. "Through the balls of my feet, I
could feel the ocean surging against the pilings below" (57).
Like the slow ticking of the clock and the slow movement of
its hands in relation to the movements of the dancer's legs,
the surf counterpoints the dance. Robert used to love the
ocean; now he hates it. Gloria observes that the waves have
been moving for a million years; it is between the rising and
falling of a wave that Robert honors her plea that he shoot
her. Robert used to dislike the sun; now he tries to absorb
every moment of sunlight that falls through a crack in the
roof of the windowless hall.

> It lasted only about ten minutes but during those
> ten minutes I moved slowly about in it (I had to
> move to keep from being disqualified) letting it
> cover me completely....
>
> I watched the triangle on the floor get smaller.
> Finally it closed altogether and started up my legs.
> It crawled up my body like a living thing. When
> it got to my chin I stood on my toes, to keep my
> head in as long as possible. I did not close my
> eyes. I kept them wide open, looking straight in-
> to the sun. It did not blind me at all. In a mo-
> ment it was gone (47-48).

One is reminded of Meursault, who says, "I've often thought
that had I been compelled to live in the trunk of a dead tree,
with nothing to do but gaze up at the patch of sky just over-
head, I'd have got used to it by degrees" (95). Gloria observes that he moves like a ballet dancer, as he follows the
dime-sized ray of sun. McCoy suggests the existential idea
that man can expect only rare moments of natural bliss.
Ironically, the brief respite, by allowing time to reflect on
its context, it sometimes too bitter, and Robert is glad when
the siren calls him back to the dance floor.

The form of this novel is strictly congruent with all
its elements. Juxtaposition is McCoy's most effective technique for controlling and conceptualizing his raw material.
Robert's story is presented as an interior monologue, the
thirteen unlucky parts of which are juxtaposed to fragments
of the sentence of death which a judge is pronouncing upon
him. On the first page a single statement directs the prisoner to stand. The next page begins as he stands up. The

ironic immediacy of the sentence lends an immediacy to
Robert's memory of the dance. The initial image is Gloria's
face the moment after Robert fires the gun; at the end, the
firing itself is depicted. Thus, the brevity of the novel gives
the impression of a single juxtaposition. The marriage ceremony on the dance floor is juxtaposed to the Lord's prayer,
which is juxtaposed to the killings in the bar. Another graphic
device is the score box that heads the last four chapters,
showing: ELAPSED HOURS. COUPLES REMAINING. As the
hours accumulate, the judge's words grow larger and larger
on the page. On the last page, he invokes God's mercy on
the prisoner's soul.

    As he tells it from the vantage of the prisoner's dock,
Robert comments briefly (in italics) on his own story. Before
he shoots Gloria, he recalls the shooting of his grandfather's
horse when Robert was a child. "I heard a shot. I still
hear that shot" (127). Thus, the present was given in the
past; the sentence he hears now, as he recalls the past, was
passed during the dance, before the murder, because it is inherent in the nature of things. McCoy's structure gives us
a sense of the simultaneity of the sentence with the conditions
that produced the "crime." Robert concludes that while the
tune varies, the dance, one's experiences, are the same:
nothing is new. Gloria says of the action of the waves,
"It's been going on for a million years" (124). The novel is
superbly compressed: Robert's meeting Gloria is briefly
described and their parting briefly depicted: the eight-hun-
dred seventy-nine hour-long dance is the large center of the
action. The brevity of the killing and of the sentence, of
the book itself, is an ironic comment on the length, the prolonged agony of the dance. It is singularly appropriate that
dance-murder-trial be compressed within the judge's sentence.

    None of McCoy's fiction is now available for the mass
    market

4.

    The tough writers lacked a doctrine which would im-
pose upon their narratives any predetermined pattern. Although Zola argued that the novelist should base his work on
careful documentation, as though he were a scientist conduct-
ing an experiment, free of moral conventions and preconceived
theories, such an assertion determined that his own dispassionate examination of phenomena would lead to conclusions
as definite as natural laws--the conclusion, for instance, that

heredity and environment determine the actions of men.   An
inverse expression of this mania to explain man's ecological
context is the psychological realism of Henry James and James
Joyce.   The detachment of the objective realist allows surface details to make their own statements; the avant-garde
extention of this method is the objectivism of Robbe-
Grillet.   Using the technique of selective realism, tough fiction achieves an objectivity that scorns romantic subjectivism
and idealization and reflects a lower-class, harsh, sordid
environment, and depicts character as a product of social
conditions, spoiling if not rotten.   Theirs is the pure vision
of the animal, which sees, but cannot (or in their case will
not) evaluate.   While too many of the proletarian writers
wrote about the masses to the intellectuals, Cain, Traven,
and other hard-boiled writers, wrote about and to the masses,
giving violent impetus to their forbidden dreams, dramatizing their darkest temptations and their basic physical drives.

Herbert J. Muller, in Modern Fiction: A Study of
Values, argues that more of an influence upon the tough
novel than Hemingway were the proletarian writers.   As an
extension of naturalism which "subordinated style to matter,"
and as "an expression of the postwar mood, with its distrust
of rhetoric," proletarian fiction gave the "tendency toward
the hard-boiled manner not only a new impetus but a new
direction."   In On Native Grounds, Alfred Kazin affirms the
relationship.   "The violence of left-wing writing all through
the thirties, its need of demonstrative terror and brutality,
relates that writing to the slick, hard-boiled novel which,
in the hands of writers like John O'Hara, James M. Cain,
Jerome Weidman, and many others, became a distinctive
contemporary fashion" (301).   In "Disengagement: The Art
of the Beat Generation," Kenneth Rexroth said: "Much of
the best popular fiction deals with the world of the utterly
disaffiliated....   The first, and still the greatest, novelist
of total disengagement is B. Traven," an "I. W. W. of
German ancestry" (35).   Traven's fiction lacks both the
strident commitment of much of the proletarians and the
seeming indifference of the tough guys to ethical implications
of human suffering.   But in some of his attitudes, in his
style, and in other characteristics of his fiction he is strikingly similar to Cain, Hammett, Chandler, and McCoy.

On publication in German in 1926, The Death Ship,
The Story of an American Sailor, was a sudden sensation and
made B. Traven famous.   But Traven also became the most
famous unknown writer.   "The creative person should," he

said, "have no other biography than his work." Even after
his death in 1969, he remained a mysterious celebrity, whose
books always sold very well in Europe. There was a revival of interest in the United States in the sixties. In B. Traven, An Introduction, Michael L. Baumann called The Death
Ship

> an attack on capitalists, nationalism, and bureau-
> cracy; its viewpoint is anarchist; its humor is
> sardonic, grim and cheerful by turns; its style is
> ironic; its hero is wise and naive, an American
> "innocent" who suffers his "fate," though he is
> fiercely indignant at the injustice of the prevailing
> social conditions. The novel's vision is tragicomic,
> deeply involved yet highly detached (117-18).

Based on the author's own experiences, written when he was
about twenty-four, The Death Ship is unique, apparently free
of direct influences, just as B. Traven is in some ways unlike any other writer, although one may sometimes think of
Celine, possibly of Henry Miller. The book may be classified
as a proletarian novel, written in the style of tough-guy fiction, but its thesis is not as doctrinaire, as deliberately
worked out as that of most proletarian novels, nor its style
as conscious as that of most tough-guy novels.

        For Gerard Gales, the young American narrator,
stranded in Antwerp when his ship returns to New Orleans
without him, the passport has displaced the sun as the center
of the universe. Unable to prove his citizenship, he is a man
without a country, and his physical presence is no official
proof of his birth. Like Kafka's K. in The Trial, he moves
through a labyrinth of bureaucracy; officials empowered to
dispense passports, certificates, sailor's-books, receipts,
affidavits, seals, and licenses conduct the inquisition of the
modern age. The war for liberty and democracy has produced a Europe in which to be hungry is human, to lack a
passport is inhuman--unless you are rich.

        A victim of nationalism, moving among fading echoes
of speeches on international brotherhood, Gerard is an in-
dividualist. Immigration officials conspire to smuggle him
back into Belgium, then into France, where he is jailed for
riding a train without a ticket and later sentenced to be shot
as a suspected spy. Ironically, when he senses the universal animosity toward Americans and pretends to be German,
he is treated royally. In Spain he is left entirely alone.

A people politically oppressed, the Spanish seem freer than
other men and Gerard loves them.   But the peasants are so
good to him that he feels useless and hates himself; he
senses the error in a Communist state where the individual
is denied the privilege of taking his own risks.   Because he
is a sailor without a ship, and because he wants to return
to his girl, Gerard signs aboard The Yorikke.

   If he once thought that the world consisted of deck-
hands and men who made paint, he descends now into sailor's
hell as a drag man in a stokehold.   Its name obscured on
the bow, The Yorikke, too, appears to lack a proper birth
certificate, but though she seems ashamed of her name,
Gerard exhibits a kind of nationalism himself when he with-
holds his true name and country and signs on as an Egyptian;
no American would sail on such a ship, and he realizes that,
despite its many faults, he loves his country and is wretch-
edly homesick.   The Yorikke resembles no ship he has ever
seen; she appears to be insane.   The ship as existential
metaphor is almost as confined as McCoy's dance floor, and
work is the dance of agony.   A model death ship, she has
no life jackets.   A death ship is so called because her owners
have decided to scuttle her for the insurance.   "A death ship
leaving a civilized port with clean papers?" (89).   The crew,
desperate men called "deads," at the end of their tether when
they come aboard, do not know when the ship will go down.
"I felt that the sea would not take this tub, which had all the
diseases known under heaven, for the simple reason that the
sea did not wish to be infected with leprosy and pus" (130).
No supplies--spoons, coffee cups, blankets--are provided;
the men repeatedly steal a single bar of soap from one another until it has been through every filthy hand; conditions
are worse than in a concentration camp.   The only thing in
ample supply is work, and if a man tries to collect overtime
on a ship pathologically committed to profits he may find himself in a black hold with rats that would terrify a cat.   Traven
conveys a vivid sense of what "she" means as pronoun for
a ship; Gerard constantly describes The Yorikke in very
intimate and telling female terms.   "I find myself falling in
love with that old Jane ...   Honest baby, I love you   ...
Grate-bars have crushed some of my toes.   And each finger-
nail has its own painful story to tell   ...   But every outcry
of pain was a love-cry for you, honey" (250).

   Gerard admires his mysterious captain whose intelligence sets him apart from the old style pirate.   He takes
care of his men, and they would rather sink with the ship

than inform the authorities that she is carrying contraband for the Riffs. The Yorikke crew is the filthiest Gerard has ever seen; the men wear bizarre rigs and rags. Some appear to have been shanghaied off the gallows. In the towns, other sailors shun them; men, women, and children fear them; and the police, afraid they may leave the town in ashes, follow them.

The filthiest member of the black gang is the drag man, who must perform extra and loathsome chores. Work is at the center of this novel--the struggle to get it, and, under extreme conditions, the horror and ultimate beauty of it. Delight in conveying an inside view is a characteristic of tough-guy literature, especially in Cain's novels. Gerard gives all the details of various work routines. One of the most horrific passages in literature is Traven's description of putting back fallen grate bars while the boiler is white hot (146-47, 153). After his first bout at what becomes a daily tasks, Gerard declares that no hell could be greater torture. "I may justly say, though, that since that night, my first night with grate-bars in the ash-pit, I feel myself standing above the gods. I am free. Unbound. I may now do whatever I wish. I may curse the gods" (153).

Gerard resurrects the freshness of the cliché that men become like machines. He feels like a gladiator for Caesar's fight-to-the-death spectacles. Bravery on the battlefield is nothing when compared to the bravery of men who do certain work to keep civilization afloat. No flag drapes the bodies of casualties; they go like garbage over the fantail. On a death ship no laws keep a man in line; each worker is crucially necessary and work is a common bond. With no sense of heroics, Gerard helps save two men and is himself saved. "My closest countryman is the one who burns his skin at the same furnace I do" (157). He does not desert because his friend Stanislav would then have to work alone. Though Traven appears to show how men grow accustomed to misery and filth, he insists that "There is no getting used to pain and suffering. You become only hardboiled, and you lose a certain capacity to be impressed by feelings" (163). Few fictive descriptions of the life, the hopes, the illusions, and attitudes of the doomed sailor, his qualities of ingenuity, improvisation, and audacity are as complete as Traven's.

Ironically, just as Gerard, despite his misery, learns to live and laugh on the ship, he senses The Yorikke's

imminent doom.   A further irony comes when Gerard and
Stanislav are shanghaied from The Yorikke to serve on the
new but disastrously slow Empress of Madagascar, which is
to be scuttled in a few days.   But The Empress kills her
plotting captain and stands like a tower between the rocks
before she sinks.   Stanislav eats like a shipowner before he
drowns.   He and Gerard are safely tied to a piece of wreck-
age, but Stanislav has a hallucination in which he sees The
Yorikke leaving the dock.   Wanting to go with her, he de-
taches himself and slips into the sea.   Not yet rescued,
Gerard pays his respects to his comrade in the last lines of
the novel.

> Stanislav had signed on for a long voyage.   For a
> very great voyage.   I could not understand this.
> How could he have signed on?   He had no sailor's
> card.   No papers whatever.   They would kick him
> off right away.
>   Yet he did not come up.   The Great Skipper
> had signed him on.   He had taken him without
> papers (287).

The style of the story--rough, garrulous, full of completely justified profanity--sounds translated, but is consistent
with Gerard's semiliterate immigrant background.   Though
these qualities become wearisome in three hundred pages, the
sheer energy of the telling achieves a special eloquence.
Traven is overtly fascinated by the way words come about;
Gerard indulges in figurative rhetoric; many of his wisecracks
seem lame, probably because his slang is dated, as some
of Cain's is now.   Humor, wit, and comedy are interwoven
quite naturally among the darks of Traven's narrative.   The
style provides an amplification of theme through the play of
language.   Although Traven does not set up satirical situations, his diction and metaphorical pretenses create a satirical distortion in telling of such episodes as those involving
bureaucracy.

No plot, no story line as such hold the novel together;
narratively, it seems split in half, but the handling of theme,
the picaresque looseness, and the personality of the narrator
create an effect appropriate to the material.   The static
quality is relieved by sudden transitions and by the frequent
use of tales and anecdotes, as in The Treasure of Sierra
Madre. Gerard is a storyteller who never tires of retelling
a tale.   The consulate scenes are repetitious; we get var-
iations on the same routine, though speeded up and fore-

shortened sometimes; and toward the end, Stanislav tells
Gerard a story about himself that closely resembles Gerard's
earlier experiences.

Gerard is especially fond of ridiculing popular fiction
and movie versions of the seafaring life; the difference between living and listening to an experience is discussed in
the beginning and at the end. "I figure I might like to change
places and rather read stories than live them.... This
helped us not to forget that we were still on high sea and not
reading a story in bed" (270). Gerard tells his general story
the way a sailor would, commenting with joking metaphors
and reflecting constantly on the meaning of events. "Yet
whoever survived" the death ship "could never be frightened
any more during his life-time by anything. For him nothing
had become impossible as long as it was within reach of a
courageous man" (185). The reader is visualized as a captive audience for a man who has at last found a way to speak
without interruption on various social, political, and economic
conditions. "Only what you talk into yourself, only that makes
you what you are" (270). The novel has some poignant moments, too, but, as is typical of Cain's and other tough-guy
novels, sentimentality occasionally intrudes.

Gerard and Stanislav are not to be associated with
the victims of recent literature. Like Frank Chambers and
Meursault, they are more victims of the nature of things
than of conditions that can be reformed. Gerard may gripe
with every breath he takes, but he does not whine. "I
won't give up and I won't give in...." (279). "But I also
knew for certain that it would not be my death ship, no matter what might happen to her.... I shall not be a gladiator
on her.... Imperator Caesar Augustus ... you have lost
one of the slaves who greet you: 'The moribund salute you,
hail!' You shall not hear me whine again.... I spit at you
and at your whole damn breed. Swallow that. I am ready
now for battle" (131). He proudly insists that he can do
work any man can do, anywhere. He contemptuously refuses
to bow to circumstance. He refuses to blame the shipowners.
"If I had jumped over the railing nobody could have made me
work in this hell. I did not jump, and by not doing it I
forsook my prime right to be my own master and my own
lord. Since I did not take my fate into my own hands, I had
no right to refuse to be used as a slave. Why do I permit
myself to be tortured? Because I have hope, which is the
blessing, the sin, and the curse of mankind" (144). He can
hope that he will be resurrected from the "deads" by this

own will and fortitude.   He knows that for the courageous man
who survives the ordeal of The Yorikke anything is possible.

By going to the bottom of agony in his daily task of
replacing grate bars, Gerard comes out with a kind of peace,
aware of his place in a universe that now has meaning in the
slightest thing.   The death ship "taught me to see the soul in
apparently life-less objects....   No more can I ever feel
alone.   I feel I am a tiny part of the universe; and if one is
missing, the universe is not complete--in fact does not exist"
(162).   This earned romanticism enables him to see beauty
in the conventionally ugly.

The intentions of the novel are uncertain; but at moments it appears to be an allegory about the laboring class.
Working unseen at sea, deep in the black hole of an ash pit,
these men who were never born, in a sense, who are without
a country, go to their deaths on a ship that does not exist
officially.   Gerard constantly speaks of the ship metaphori-
cally as being over five thousand years old.   The flag is so
dirty it could represent any country, and thus represents all.
Many nationalities are represented among the crew; each
nameless person is called, ironically, by the name of the
country he claims, but which has denied his existence.

Although Gerard covers, directly to the reader and in
dialogue, almost every grievance of the laborer of the first
twenty-five years of this century, he is not interested in easy
working conditions and fringe benefits.   Repeatedly, he preach-
es the gospel of hard work, not because work is good for the
soul, which seems less involved than muscle, but because it
is good for man the animal.   Unlike other proletarian writers,
Traven achieves a kind of mystique about work.

As in McCoy's novel, one thinks of Camus' Sisyphus:
for his disobedience of the officials, Sisyphus was condemned
to the futile task of rolling a huge rock to the top of the
mountain, after which it rolled back down to the plain.   "They
had thought with some reason that there is no more dreadful
punishment than futile and hopeless labor" (88).   Camus likened this labor to that of the proletariat.   Unintentionally,
perhaps, Traven has translated Sisyphus' mythic task into
existential reality.

147,896

College of St. Francis Library
Joliet, Illinois

John Garfield, Lana Turner and Cecil Kellaway in The Post-man Always Rings Twice (1946).

CHAPTER TWO

Cain's Career as a Novelist

In the teens, twenties and thirties, Cain worked as editor of The Lorraine Cross (a weekly for the Allied Expeditionary Forces), as a reporter on The Baltimore Sun, as teacher of mathematics at Washington College, where his father was president, as instructor of journalism at St. John's College, and as editorial writer for Walter Lippmann on The New York World. He wrote articles, mostly political, interpreting the American scene for The Atlantic, The American Mercury, The Nation, The New Yorker, The Saturday Evening Post, Esquire, and Vanity Fair. Gang wars, union strife, and individual crimes of passion must have encouraged him to view American history as a long panorama of violence. Like Hemingway, Cain sharpened his vision in the midst of events, as when he reported on labor violence from the coalfields of West Virginia. Showing the spirit, if not the influence, of Mencken and Sinclair Lewis, and of William Bolitho and Alexander Woollcott, who also wrote for the World, Cain's essays were iconoclastic, satirical, and cynical. For his raw, raw material, a jabbing, slicing prose and a tough tone seemed appropriate. As a journalist, Cain observed the tough-guy mystique, recorded it in newspaper and magazine articles and editorials, then transformed it into myth in stories, plays, and novels.

In his essays and in the dialogues collected in Our Government, a rather controversial work (1930), Cain examined the clichés of the union boss, the politician, the preacher, the pedagogue, the editorial writer. These clichés, he observed, often came out of the American's compulsion toward self-dramatization. The unheroic quality of democracy is obvious in such people as the "servists," whom he analyzed in an essay called "The Pathology of Service," the purpose of which was "to isolate the bacillus of Service." The disease originates in the appetite of dull people for drama. In the short story, "Pastorale" the

American's need for self-dramatization betrays a man into
confessing murder. As a young man, Cain admired the py-
rotechnics of power, preferring "cynics" of the past (Napoleon was his favorite) to America's colorless public men,
who lacked heroic lustre.

Cain published his first short story, "Pastorale," in
1928 when he was thirty-six. He was forty-two when his
first novel, The Postman Always Rings Twice, was published
in 1934. Knopf rejected it, but Walter Lippmann, who, during an automobile trip he and Cain took to see the sights of
Southern California, had asked to see it, praised it, and
asked permission to submit it to Macmillan. It was again
rejected. Lippmann finally persuaded his friend Knopf to
publish it, however, at a somewhat reduced advance.
Blanche Knopf tells a different story. She reports that the
MS "came in practically over the transom, accompanied by
the warning that if Knopf didn't decide within 24 hours, the
book would go elsewhere. 'I bought it without reading it,
I think'" ("50 Years of the Borzoi," 54). "She was wrong,"
says Cain. "Under the contract, Knopf had 30 days to make
up his mind, and took 29." When the book came out it
caused a sensation.

Its original title was Bar-B-Q, which Knopf hated, and
which Cain decided to change to The Postman Always Rings
Twice, which Knopf hated even more. He and other persons
wrote to Cain pleading for another title, urging For Love or
Money. But Cain liked The Postman Always Rings Twice
and stuck with it. In the Preface to Three of a Kind (1943)
he relates the origin of his title. He was talking with his
playwright friend Vincent Lawrence one day about Lawrence's
nervousness while waiting to hear from a producer about a
play. "I almost went nuts. I'd sit and watch for the postman, and then I'd think 'You got to cut this out,' and then
when I left the window I'd be listening for his ring ... he'd
always ring twice," so Lawrence would know it was the postman. Cain interrupted Lawrence's "harrowing tale" to declare
that he had given him the title for his novel. "Say, he rang
twice for Chambers, didn't he?" "That's the idea." "And
on that second ring, Chambers had to answer, didn't he?
Couldn't hide out in the backyard any more." "His number
was up, I'd say." "I like it." "Then that's it."

For Cain, the postman, whose custom is always to
ring twice, rang thrice. This first novel is one of America's all-time best sellers and has gone through a great many
editions; Cain adapted it to the stage; it was adapted for

motion pictures twice.   After a half century, the novel is
still casting a spell in over sixteen languages, both as popular entertainment and as a work of art of a very peculiar
sort, respected, with qualifications, by students of literature.

     With the success of the novel, Cain sold many short
stories that had not attracted attention before, though even
in 1931, before he left New York for Hollywood, magazines--
Collier's, for instance--were always "discovering" him.   He
published a story in The Ladies' Home Journal, four in Liberty, and two in Redbook.

     In his Preface to Three of a Kind, Cain said, "These
novels, though written fairly recently, really belong to the
Depression, rather than the war, and make interesting foot-
notes to an era. "   All three ran, in shorter form, as serials
in Liberty. Cain wrote Double Indemnity (1936) to get money
to finance the continued run of his play version of The Postman. In addition to his own experience selling insurance,
Cain obtained background information for this story by talking with his father, who had become a vice president of a
Baltimore insurance company; Cain got a glimpse of the in-
trigues at the top of a company like that.   But the story itself had its inception in an anecdote of Arthur Krock's at
lunch one day at the World. When Krock was managing editor of the Louisville Courier-Journal, he experienced the
horror of a particularly obscene, though funny "typo. "   He
finally forced the truth out of the terrified printer: "Mr. Krock,
you do nothing, your whole life, but watch to head it off,
something like that happening. And then, and then, Mr.
Krock, you catch yourself watching for chances. "   The anecdote lingered with Cain, until it occurred to him that if instead of a printer, an insurance salesman, figured in it.
there would be "dynamite" in the idea.   "This agent spent
his whole life on his guard against people trying to crook
the company, and then found himself looking for chances--
and an accomplice.   She turned up pretty soon in the person
of a woman slightly fed up with her husband. "   The title was
suggested by James Geller, Cain's agent.

     Career in C Major (1938) originally began as a story
about a successful woman, a buyer in a department store,
whose husband could never make a success of anything.

          She was really decent, not throwing it up to him at all,
          loving him, impressing her friends, and all the rest of
          it. Then, by accident, he is found to have a voice.

His failure had only endeared him to her,   but his
success she couldn't take.   It wasn't that she be-
grudged him, but being second banana simply stood
her on her head.   This conception didn't work.
Then I came around to the idea I finally wrote, but
that didn't work either: a woman wanting a career
and not being able to have it seemed a 100% ninny.
But then, on New Year's Day, 1937, I thought, why
not make her a bitch?   I did, and the thing went
down with no trouble.   It took me 28 days, until
then a record for me.

The story originally appeared under the title "Two Can Sing."
In 1949, The Embezzler appeared in Liberty as "Money and
the Woman."

        Serenade (1938) began in a conversation with Dr. Town-
send just after Cain's ill-starred venture into music, when he
tried to become an opera singer as his mother had been, and
twenty years before it was written.   Townsend's fascination
with the idea lingered with Cain.   It was to be the tale of a
singer who would commit a crime, probably murder, escape,
and then not be able to open his mouth for fear of giving himself away.   As the years went by, it seemed more workable
that someone else, probably a girl, should commit the crime,
and somewhere along the line, after visits to Agua Caliente,
during Cain's Hollywood sojourn, she became Mexican.   "Then
the homosexual angle got into it.   Then it seemed to me that
only two people might possibly understand the implications of
it--a psychiatrist, who simply seemed dull; or, a prostitute,
who knows all about men, especially their offbeat characteristics.   So the Mexican girl became a Mexican whore."
But for years, he held off writing it, feeling it too pat,
clinically.   However, all Cain needed was the go-ahead from
a man in the know, and he got this one night in Hollywood at
the home of Samson Raphaelson, the playwright and screenwriter.   There he told Dr. Samuel Hirshfeld, a prominent
Los Angeles physician, the story, and when the doctor asked
why Cain didn't write it, Cain replied that he didn't want to
do a book a doctor might laugh at.   The effect of homosexuality on a man's singing voice might not be clinically sound.
Hirshfeld said he wasn't laughing; he found the idea one of
the most interesting he had ever heard.   So Cain wrote
Serenade. He later heard that it was prescribed reading in
psychiatry courses all over the country.   "You," said Dr.
James M. Neilson, a Los Angeles psychiatrist, "found one

that Kraft-Ebbing missed, that's all.   That's why the book
has kicked up such excitement."

Having written <u>Career</u> and <u>Serenade</u> the year before,
and having written <u>The Modern Cinderella</u> (The Root of His
Evil) and a play in 1938, the year his father died, Cain,
finding that he was utterly written out, took time off to go
with his wife, Elina, to Europe, where he visited Scandinavia,
England, and Ireland.

In <u>Mildred Pierce</u> (1941) Cain presents a detailed picture of the Depression's middle-class and one of its most
convincing female archetypes, Mildred.   In <u>The Moth</u> (1948),
he deliberately presents a detailed picture of the life of the
hobo, the migrant worker.   These two novels, in many sec-
tions, come closer to the proletarian writing of the thirties
than to the tough-guy school.   Cain's twelfth book in four-
teen years, <u>The Moth</u> appeared when he was fifty-six years
old.   This story had its inception on many trips Cain used
to take, from Hollywood to Burbank, a suburb of Los Angeles, where he lived from 1932 to 1934.   The road from
Warner Brothers' studio to the main street of Burbank led
past a railroad station at the edge of town, and here,
night after night, Cain was held up by a freight.   As he
waited he often saw, silhouetted against the Verdugo Hills,
heads on tops of the cars--not just two or three, but hun-
dreds of tramps.   He used to think with horror of the human
beings up there, with no place to lay their heads, nothing to
eat, "no gleam of anything in their lives--all through no fault
of their own."   And gradually he felt he might write a book
about it.

> To get up the dope, I went to great lengths, going
> to the missions on Los Angeles street, and finally
> connecting with a mentor, a tutor, a guide to Hobo-
> hemia who was willing, for a consideration to take
> me in hand and teach me.   Moran turned out to
> be a discovery, one of the most erudite men I ever
> met.   I was baffled at his literary knowledge, until
> one day Moran explained as we rode around in my
> car, a bit sheepishly: "Look, you gotta have some-
> where to park your feet, to get warm, to sit.   So
> the Public Library is free.   So that's where the
> hobo lives--and little by little, as they won't just
> let you sit there, you do a lot of reading."

The book was an effort to let the Great Depression happen
to one man.   This simple intention might have produced one

of Cain's finest short novels, but, strangely, certain apparently autobiographical elements pertaining to his childhood entered into his conception and delayed the novel's thrust into the Depression material.

Less directly, Cain's other novels of the forties reflect their decade: Love's Lovely Counterfeit (1942), Past All Dishonor (1946), Sinful Woman (1947), and The Butterfly (1947); in The Butterfly he finally realized his minefield material. It is difficult to disassociate the aura of the movie versions made during the forties of Cain's novels of the thirties from one's sense of the times as evoked by the novels then coming out.

In Cain's novels of the early forties, there is almost no sense of a war going on. Two novels dealt with things remote in time or geography: Past All Dishonor, set during the Civil War; The Butterfly, set up the creeks of the West Virginia mountains. In his Preface to the British omnibus volume Three of Hearts (1949), he says: "These novels will come as a surprise to readers of my previous works, for there is a never-never-land quality in all of them; a flight, not so much from reality as from actuality, not to be found in any of my previous work." Although the time is the present in The Butterfly, a lean, stark tale of incest and moonshine, set in Harlan County, it "develops aspects of the inhabitants which are local, inbred, and individual, and were just as tragic in the eighteenth century as they are now. Each story, in its own way, recoils from the present as it existed at the time it was written" (v-x).

While Cain was writing his tough, present-day novels, Edna Ferber, Walter D. Edmunds, Ernest Boyd, Margaret Mitchell, Hervey Allen, Kenneth Roberts were establishing the historical genre that became very popular in the forties with Frank Yerby, Thomas B. Costain, Van Wyck Mason, and Kathleen Winsor. If novelists seduce audiences, audiences also seduce novelists. In Past All Dishonor, Cain answered to that interest in historical fiction, while infusing his novel with elements of the tough-guy fiction for which he was famous. The novel evokes the Civil War era in the same economical way his modern novels evoke modern times. Double Indemnity in historical dress, Past All Dishonor was, as reviewers noted, very unlike Forever Amber and other historical novels of those years.

Cain is interested in the past for its own sake. His intention in his historical novels is summed up in his com-

ment on the jacket of Past All Dishonor: "I have tried to
present the life of the time as it was." Speaking of Mignon,
Cain sees the dictates of the period novel as rigidly set.
"The given events ... can't be changed, of course, as to
wind, weather, tide, or number of soldiers killed ... It
becomes indeed a sort of etude in algebra to fit the characters to the events, with no possible relation to proper narrative, so you come out with something that looks like fiction,
and with luck may be mistaken for it." He said that it had
been "a long, dreary pull. I had read of writers who took
years, and did draft after draft after draft, on some period
novel, and thought of course that couldn't be me." Then he
is moved to vow: "I shall never, as long as I live, try a
period novel again. It is like a sentence in the penitentiary
... you refuse to leave your cell until your time is up, by
then having come to the point you must finish ... even if
it's not so much by the time you get done" (Letter to Madden). After Mignon was published, he said of such novels,
"All that reading and labor, and a kind of mouse is born"
(Nichols, "Postman's Assistant," 8).

        Cain presents an odd argument for writing about things
remote from the war. With a war going on, it was difficult,
Cain strangely assumes, for a writer to write as he was accustomed to "of this time, this place, and this world." The
search for what he calls "firmer footing" led to an "increased
output of period novels that began to be marked in the early
1940s" (Three of Hearts).

        His first break with the immediate scene was Love's
Lovely Counterfeit. What seemed in 1941 "a gay idea,"
seasoned with malice, to write of some "highly amusing skull-
duggeries around my home city," L.A., "suddenly seemed
somehow a dirty trick." Therefore, he set the story in a
fictitious midwestern town so he would at least have "nothing
very grievous" on his conscience. "By 1942 anything current had become a complete impossibility, and like many of
my colleagues I turned the calendar back many years to find
a time when at least the values that men cherished were fixed.
and comprehensible: So he wrote Past All Dishonor and
The Butterfly as being "unassociated with the perplexities
then plaguing us" (Three of Hearts). One wonders which
writers he considers his colleagues; Cain's attitude is perhaps that of the commerical writer whose values and assumptions differ from writers like Farrell, Faulkner, Warren,
Ira Wolfert, Bellow, and Wright Morris, who wrote novels
during the war and who did not feel that to take a glancing

look at the contemporary American scene was a way of
supporting the war.

Cain displayed both a sort of social consciousness,
stimulated perhaps by the war, and a characteristic toughness when, in 1946, he set out to organize all the writers
in America into an American Author's Authority (a similar
effort got under way in 1981). Cain approached the project
with all of the great energy, sense of authority, arrogance,
and drama of one of his characters. By 1948, the effort
had failed. And he had married Florence Macbeth, Chicago
opera singer he had long admired; they left Hollywood for
Hyattsville, Maryland, near Washington, where he wanted to
research Mignon, a Civil War novel. He never left there.

In the fifties not much was heard from Cain. He
wrote Jealous Woman (1950); The Root of His Evil was finally published in 1951. His own serious struggle with diet-
ing for his health inspired the half-autobiographical Galatea,
(1953), a tale of a fat girl, her prize-ring trainer boyfriend,
and her resturant-keeper husband. It was not well-received.
Then for ten years Cain was silent.

In a Newsweek interview, he spoke of having been ill
from 1957 to 1962. "I wasn't worth a damn" ("Cain Scrutiny,"
99). But in 1962 Cain got back to work on Mignon. Into
this novel he put ten years of research on the cotton racket
during the Civil War; but the elements would not cohere.
Originally he was attracted to the idea that "the war between
the Union and Secesh was nothing compared to the war between the army and navy during the Red River Expedition."
For Civil War enthusiasts, Mignon (1963) might be an exciting adventure-mystery tale. Dramatizing the Red River Expedition, the bloody battles around Alexandria, and the cotton
conspiracy of 1864, Cain begins his story in Mardi Gras
New Orleans, then shifts up the Mississippi onto Red River.
"It seemed a promising thing, just up my alley, with sardon-
ic overtones and everything I like to deal with," he comment-
ed. "But though I finally got the book out, I didn't pull it
off. It was the most ill-starred venture I ever embarked
on" (Letter to Madden).

At seventy-three, Cain published The Magician's Wife
(1965). Modeled on The Postman, it was received with contempt. This story had no special starting idea beyond Cain's
desire to write a story about a masculine, average guy in
the meat business. Clay Lockwood might have received the

Jaycees' Man of the Year Award had the magician's wife not
lured him onto the end of a plank by involving him in her
scheme to collect her husband's insurance payoff (<u>Double In-
demnity</u> again).   Within striking distance of money and murder, the woman secretes a peculiar ordor, more than faintly
suggestive of a rattlesnake.   "It wasn't too good an effort,"
Cain admitted.   He could not end what he had started, and
the suicide was a bad move, an "ending few readers could accept.
The ending of a tale carries or should carry its point, and
this story didn't seem to have one.   But it's a hit in Japan,
where hari-kari is an honorable way out!" (Letter to Madden).

Until he died in 1977 at the age of eighty-five, Cain
lived in a frame house on a quiet Hyattsville street.   In
1967, he was working on two novels.   One was totally different from his previous books, concerning the psychological
conflict between a little girl who is given a tiger cub to raise
and her domineering mother who refuses to allow the child to
do it in her own way.   The other novel in progress, he said,
derived from his stock in trade.   The first remains in manuscript.   The second may have been <u>Rainbow's End</u> (1975).
When twenty-two year old Davey Howell discovers that an
airplane highjacker has parachuted into his isolated rural
southeast Ohio solitude with $100,000, he faces a greed-lust-
moral crisis complicated by his love of the beautiful steward-
ess hostage and his incestuous love of his mother.

One of the few major writers of the thirties still at
work, Cain created, at eighty-four, the best of his more recent novels.   <u>The Institute</u> (1976) does not have the force
that made Cain the most powerful of the tough-guy writers,
but he is still in command of all his most effective qualities.
The story Lloyd Palmer tells fits the classic Cain formula
The Cain hero always meets and "rapes" his female equal
in the first few chapters, then the two become partners in
a great adventure, forcing a then shared wish to come true.
A former football hero, Palmer is a scholar who needs
twenty-two million dollars to establish a national institute
of biography.   Richard Garrett has the money and is married
to the "girl."   This combination of characters and circumstances produces violent complications.   And in <u>The Institute,</u>
we watch him handle familiar elements in new and fascinating
combinations.   For instance, like several other Cain heroes,
Palmer is an egotistical, know-it-all braggart, full of detailed
knowledge about not only his specialty, biography, but
many other subjects as well.   And he makes us eager to
learn the mysterious procedures involved in setting up a

twenty-two million dollar institute and his improvised methods of dealing with myriad problems that arise.   Those procedures are as suspenseful as his dangerous love affair.
One of the novel's problems is the out-dated tone of much of
the conversation.   The time may as well be the twenties.
Similar problems of style, of anachronisms, plagued Rainbow's End, but they are less disruptive here.   All Cain's
best qualities keep uneasy company with faults that come
naturally when one is no longer in the midst of the action,
watching, and listening.

CHAPTER THREE

Cain and the Movies of the
Thirties and Forties

As Dillinger walked toward the woman in red, thus
signaling his own execution in the streets, Clark Gable, on
the screen of Chicago's Biograph Theater, was walking to
the electric chair in <u>Manhattan Melodrama</u>. Popular culture
expressed the spontaneity of violence in America, and the
public was eager, even while condemning it as evil, to experience it vicariously. On this craving for blood, the American detective story has long thrived. (Our first literary
export, it was immediately domesticated by the English; ironically, in the guise of James Bond--a "cool" version of Mike
Hammer--England has assimilated the charateristics of our
myth of masculine exploits and exported to us our own bill
of goods.) On a higher level of intention, proletarian fiction
also contributed to the atmosphere of violence. That the
American's appetite for violence is stronger than his preten-
sion to the refinements of civilization is clearly evident in
popular culture. Cain has studied, some say cynically ex-
ploited, this trait in American character.

During Cain's New York years, the theater projected
the tough attitude: <u>The Hairy Ape, Front Page, The Petrified
Forest, Waiting for Lefty, Winterset, Dead End</u>. Although
he had little success with his other plays, Cain's adaptation
of <u>The Postman</u> did fairly well on Broadway in 1936. From
his friend Philip Goodman, the New York producer, he learned
about dramatic tension and narrative technique. But his
greatest teacher of writing was Vincent Lawrence, former
playwright, hard drinker, free spender, typical American
tough guy, who hammered out highly successful movie scripts.

James M. Cain went to Hollywood in 1931 and stayed
about ten years; he was not a successful scriptwriter, but he
claims to have learned a good deal from his experience in
the movies, and from other movie people. Critics think well

of the movies made from his novels, but they accuse him of
of showing in his novels negative effects of the medium.   To
understand Cain, his work, and the tough-guy genre in general, Cain should be studied in relation to the movies.   The
tough-guy novel and its movie counterpart have cross-fertilized
each other.   Not only have classic gangster movies been
made from tough novels, but most of the best tough writers
have worked for Hollywood.   Dashiell Hammett, Raymond
Chandler, and Horace McCoy were among Hollywood's more
successful screenwriters, financially when not artistically.
Made into celebrated movies were: Hammett's The Maltese
Falcon (1940), The Thin Man (1934), The Glass Key (1942);
Chandler's The Big Sleep (1947), Farewell, My Lovely (as
Murder My Sweet) (1946), The Lady in the Lake (1947);
Traven's The Treasure of Sierra Madre (1947); McCoy's
Kiss Tomorrow Goodbye (1950) and They Shoot Horses, Don't
They? (1969).   Essential to tough-guy movies and novels is
speed of impact.   The short tough novel, like a movie, may
be experienced in one sitting; like the movies, tough novels
are true to our fast-moving culture; the pace in movies can
be even more engrossing than well-paced stage drama.   And,
as Edmund Wilson has pointed out, many serious novelists
who don't write for the movies have been influenced by their
pace, themes, characters, tone, and attitudes.   He cites
The Grapes of Wrath and For Whom the Bell Tolls as examples ("Boys," 49n).

     Traven was not a screenwriter, but James Agee tells
a fascinating story of Traven's probable participation in the
filming of The Treasure of Sierra Madre (first published in
1927).   Hammett and Chandler were two of Hollywood's highest paid writers.   City Streets (1931) was perhaps Hammett's
best screen effort.   Chandler's adaptation of Cain's Double
Indemnity (1944) and his own original The Blue Dahlia (1946)
were the years' sensations.   Both McCoy and Cain, beginning
in 1931, were screenwriters before their first novels appeared
McCoy was successful, Cain was a failure.

     The best tough novels were written by some of the
finest screenwriters.   In Dashiel Hammett's The Maltese
Falcon (1929), Horace McCoy's They Shoot Horses, Don't
They? (1935), Raymond Chandler's The Big Sleep (1939),
and Cain's Glendale novels, one relatively neglected area
of the American fictional landscape--California (Hollywood in
particular)--was presented in images as authentic and expressive as those in the novels of Huxley, West, Schulberg,
Fitzgerald, and Waugh.

The California evoked by Cain, Hammett, Chandler, and McCoy stays with us in the way that the movies of the late thirties and early forties do. Penelope Houston, in trying to describe the appeal of these movies, concludes her analysis of The Big Sleep and other such films of violence that "epitomize an era" with: "One remembers the films rather for their settings--the detective's office, with the neon light flicking off and on across the street, the sweltering conservatory in which only the desiccated old millionaire can breathe in comfort, the gun battles in the car headlights and the sad little man (Elisha Cook, Jr., that prototype of sad little men) dying among the office filing cabinets" (The Contemporary Cinema, 67).

Hung over in the thirties, the disillusionment of the roaring twenties produced a public skepticism that welcomed a cycle of gangster films. Underworld (1927), directed by von Sternberg, written by Ben Hecht, was the first movie to present the gangster as a sympathetic type; even when later movies did not set out to portray the gangster sympathetically, audiences often responded as though the gangster were a folk hero. Underworld started a trend of gangster and tough movies that continued, with varying degrees of vigor, into the late fifties.

Little Caesar (1931) and Scarface (1932) set the style; they were the classic gangster films of the thirties. In 1934, the Legion of Decency combatted crime films so effectively that they were rare until revived in '37. Warner Brothers produced more of these movies than any other company; John Houston scripted four and directed three. Bogart starred in six of the important ones from 1936 to 1947. Other actors who set the style were Chester Morris, Wallace Beery, George Raft, Pat O'Brien, Spencer Tracy, James Cagney, Edward G. Robinson, Paul Muni, William Powell, Alan Ladd, Fred MacMurray, Dick Powell, Zachary Scott, and John Garfield. Lauren Bacall, Joan Crawford, Barbara Stanwyck, Lana Turner, Veronica Lake, Glenda Farrell, Jean Harlow, Joan Bennett, and Ida Lupino were a few of the faces and figures that decorated this masculine world with its smell of gun oil, its metallic surfaces. Readers of tough writers now had actors like Bogart to cast in the main roles as they read.

These novels and movies reflected one aspect of the national spirit of the times. People were fascinated by the glamorous gangster who in fighting to triumph over the

limitations of his environment always lost, but who made for
everyone a momentary show of toughness.   At home and
abroad, the tough guy became the American image.   With
his fast car and tommy gun, he resembled the cowboy with
his fast horse and sixshooter.   But the cowboy was a folk
hero of the distant, romantic past; the gangster, taking on a
romanticism with a hard metallic sheen, was the man of the
hour; if the cowboy offered escape from the Depression, the
gangster mastered, if only for the hour, conditions the average American felt helpless to control.   "Essentially, " says
Penelope Houston, "the people who made these films moved
about easily in the world of their shabby subjects. "   These
movies "were romantically tough but not soft-centered, like
some of the movies that followed, in which criminals pined
for the quiet country life (Asphalt Jungle) and psychiatry rode
the range.... " (66-67).

     A representative sampling of commentary on the gang-
ster or tough movies by film critics reveals a tendency to
see more significance in these movies than censors, disdain-
ful literary critics, and, certainly, the ordinary moviegoers
were inclined to see.   Parker Tyler, stylistically the R. P.
Blackmur of film critics (he often reviewed films for The
Kenyon Review), and a poet and filmmaker as well, made a
Freudian scrutiny of "The Good Villain and the Bad Hero" in
Hollywood Hallucination as early as 1944.   "The Hollywood
gangster hero has often been a bad man sugared with the
sanctity of vulgar sentimentality ...   an 'unethical' sinner,
he does not deviate through principle but through some
muffled necessity ... suicide is the precise metaphysic
which governs the moral flavor of gangster sagas. "   The
art of the gangster movie is hollow because the "moral
experience" and a "sense of the nature of crime" are
lacking.

     The similarity between a Cain tough hero and the
heroes of the hard-boiled detective genre is suggested by
Tyler's analysis of Bogart-Spade.

          Thus, cast in the orthodox temperamental mold of
          the gangster hero, the good villain Spade avoids
          being sentimentalized because of an ambivalent or-
          thodoxy--an ambivalence that permits him to have
          sympathy or contempt for his clients, and also
          friendship or hatred for the police. Thus he is an
          ideal example of the visible metamorphosis of good
          villain into bad hero, and capable as well of jug-
          gling these categories while he is in action....
          It is within the essential plot, not only of the movie

but of his character, that The Maltese Falcon should
be a phony.... (100-135).

Four years later, Robert Warshow, goes beyond
Tyler's analysis, which at the time must have seemed rather
esoteric, to endow the gangster hero in particular with grand-
er significance.   In "The Gangster as Tragic Hero," a
chapter in his brilliant The Immediate Experience, Warshow
makes the imaginative, somewhat Jungian claim that gangster
movies, like jazz, the Marx Brothers, and the hopelessness
of soap opera, are unconscious, pessimistic protests against
the forced optimism of a society in collapse.   They give us
a "modern sense of tragedy."   "The experience of the gangster as an experience of art is universal to Americans," expressing "that part of the American psyche which rejects the
qualities and the demands of modern life, which rejects
'Americanism' itself."   The gangster film embodies the dilemma of the American character "in the person of the gangster and resolves it by his death ... because it is his
death, not ours.   We are safe; for the moment, we can ac-
quiesce in our failure, we can choose to fail" (50-54).

James T. Farrell, a man whose social impulses led
him to attack the American dilemma directly in his fiction
and to ambush it in his literary criticism, reacted in 1947
against the serious consequences of tolerance toward tough-
guy fiction and movies.

> If this new movietone realism continues to flourish,
> it will probably further debauch popular taste in
> America.   One of the major virtues of serious
> realism is that it describes the pitiless force of
> circumstance and the equally pitiless drive of human
> emotions which often play so central a role
> in causing the tragic destruction of human
> beings.

But in pseudorealism these drives and forces are "replaced by the fortuitousness of automobile accidents and
the like and by a melodramatically simplified conception of
good girls and bad girls."   He seems blind to the ambigui-
ties that bemuse Tyler and Warshow.   He forsees that these
novels and movies will incense the censors.   "Then the Hollywood movietone realists will crawl back to the usual mo-
tion-picture defense of virtue.   Then they will be in a position to claim that they have tried realism, have tried to
produce serious art, and have been thwarted by powerful

forces beyond their control." The irony will be that "not
only will serious realism be open to fresh attack, but it will
also be held responsible for, and called upon to defend, movietone realism" (Literature and Morality, 146).

John Howard Lawson, another social-minded critic.
carried similar sentiments over into 1964. He deplored the
callous treatment of crime without the moral concern for
suffering and guilt that Kafka and Camus, for instance, showed
"These American examples of the film noir"--The Maltese Falcon, Double Indemnity, The Big Sleep--"have technical virtuosity, but they reduce all human feelings to a dead
level of psychotic brutality. This had been a major trend in
the U.S. during the past twenty years. The psychopathic
killer has become a familiar and often 'sympathetic' figure
on the American Screen." Lawson coscripted Algiers (1938)
with Cain.

2.

When Sharp in Serenade says, "Understand, for my
money, no picture is any good, really any good," he sums
up James M. Cain's lifelong attitude. Cain's judgment of
the movies was formed when he attended the "Nickelodeon"
with Kent Roberts Greenfield, his boyhood friend from Chestertown, Maryland in 1906. These "two intellectual snobs"
laughed themselves into "stiches" over it, not in enjoyment,
but derision, and came out feeling very superior, "perhaps
with good reason," says Cain. They had seen a comedy in
which John Bunny played a chiropodist removing a bunion.
The screams of laughter in the audience came from Bunny's
pantomime at the smell of the foot the bunion was on. They
were disgusted by the comedy short, but utterly appalled by
the feature, The Great Train Robbery. "It never occurred
to either of us that this was history of a sort, that it was
good, or that it was anything but a proper subject of scorn
from two young intellectuals, who of course knew what was
good" (Letter to Madden).

Yet, Cain insists, the contempt that he shared with
Roberts was honest contempt. "And it never has left me.
It explains, I think, more than anything else, why I flopped
in Hollywood. I wanted the picture money, I worked like a
dog to get it, I parked my pride, my aesthetic convictions,
my mind outside on the street, and did everything to be a
success at this highly paid trade" (Letter to Madden).

Cain speaks only once of taking this sort of approach to fiction.

> I studied the 'Technique' as I called it, of moving
> pictures. I did everything to become adept at them.
> The one thing I could not park was my nose. I
> could still see John Bunny in that short, still re-
> coil from his gag. My dislike of pictures went down
> to my guts, and that's why I couldn't possibly write
> them (Letter to Madden).

In the last two decades of his life, Cain saw movies only on
TV, and then only to see a "well-liked face"; he hadn't been
in a movie theater in ten or fifteen years. Why, he didn't
know, for his theoretical objections to the medium didn't account for his dislike of it. He had equally cogent objections
to the circus, or TV, or grand opera, but saw these forms
all the time, and pleasurably. Cain had little patience with
failure. To fail, as he did, in the early stages of prepara-
tion to become a singer was one thing--singing is a high art;
but to fail at a low form of entertainment, the movies, was
degrading.

Cain left for Hollywood on Armistice Day 1931, after
a call on D. A. Doran, the West Coast Studio's representative
in the Paramount offices in New York. Cain arrived in Los
Angeles in a driving rainstorm, and his first glimpse of the
city included a man in a boat, rowing around under some
palm trees. Fred Kohlmar, a novice with the William Morris
agency who later became an important producer, took him to
the Hollywood Knickerbocker, "the best hotel I have memory
of." Next day, Kohlmar took him to the studio, a place as
strange to Cain as the man in the boat under the palm trees,
and turned him over to Percy Heath, the story editor. At
that time, Cain recalls, Hollywood regarded the script as an
inescapable, but loathsome evil, and approached it according-
ly. "The director was still king, and thought if the actors
were going to speak, they had to know what to say; this king,
this dictator, still regarded himself as the creative one, who
would decide on what story to tell, and so on. So, as a pre-
liminary nuisance, this overworked story editor would work
with the writers on scripts, with all writers, believe it or
not, and then when their work was done turn their product
over to the director who would then make a movie out of it"
(Letter to Madden).

The system worked very badly, Cain says, because in

addition to driving the story editor very close to a nervous
breakdown, it resulted in all scripts being alike. But that
didn't bother the executives, who still had an obsessive idea
that action, what the camera delivered, was the essence of
pictures, the sound track, including the dialogue, being incidental. The cliché was "We're talking 'em to death. "

Cain was shocked to discover that Heath had read none
of his writings; he couldn't understand how Heath expected to
get good work out of his writers if he never read their published stories. But everything in Hollywood, to Cain, was
done on a lunatic basis. Thus, a hard-boiled writer was giv-
en a remake of De Mille's Ten Commandments as his first
assignment. In the original it was "one of the big hits of all
time, " and that seemed to be all that anyone thought worth
knowing. "That it stank, that it was glaring, monstrous piece
of slimy, phoney hokum, seemed to make no difference" (Letter to Madden). In fact, Cain wondered if anyone in the studio was capable to taking its measure. With Sam Mintz, a
writer he came to like, he went to work on this "masterpiece
of hokum"--and before Christmas had "flopped. "

Then Cain sat around for three months, waiting to be
assigned. In April, he was suddenly put on a picture called
Hot Saturday, from a novel by Harvey Ferguson. He heard
little of his efforts on this one, but presently was "closed
out, " and then faced the reality of his impulsive switch to
pictures; he was a flop, he had no income (except what he
might pick up from magazine writing), he had moved lock,
stock, and barrel to California, and had no idea what was
next.

After publication of The Postman Always Rings Twice,
written in Burbank in 1933, short stories of Cain's that the
agent couldn't sell before were cleared out overnight, and
MGM hired him to do a movie. The deal was ten thousand
dollars, one third to be paid down, one third when the story
was submitted, and one third when adjustments had been made
to studio specifications. But feeling that the assignment was
getting nowhere, Cain, to release himself from his obligation,
returned the down payment. It was months before his check
was cashed, because there was no way, as accountancy stood
then in Hollywood, Cain learned, to book the return of money
paid to an author. (So much for the self-righteous, often re-
peated charge that Cain sold out to the movies.) The film
was to be called The Duchess of Delmonico and was to have
starred Jeanette MacDonald. Cain's effort had one curious

side effect. In Goldfield for background, Cain was told by
a mining expert: "The gold here fooled them all, including
the best mining brains of the country. They found out what
they'd forgotten--that gold is where you find it." This apo-
thegm so intrigued him that he put it in the wire for Nacio
Herb Brown and Arthur Freed, who were supposed to do the
songs. Not too long afterward the song came out, "Love Is
Where You Find It," pleasing Cain a great deal.

Cain credits the movies with having taught him certain
technical devices. Though critics overemphasize their charge
of negative influences, Cain's fiction does have positive cinematic characteristics. In the four years he spent on movie
lots, he accumulated only three fractional script credits:
Stand Up and Fight (1939), with Charles Bickford and Robert
Taylor; Algiers, 1938, which made a star of Hedy Lamarr,
and costarred Charles Boyer, MGM--a stupid and feeble remake of Pepe Le Moko, according to Paul Rotha, but it got
four academy awards; Gypsy Wildcat, 1944, Universal, hokum
starring exotic Maria Montez. Cain wrote few originals; he
was mostly a script doctor, a rewrite man. None of his full
scripts reached the projection booth.

In "Camera Obscura," an important essay, well-written
to high Cain standards in the hard-boiled manner he finds so
natural, he expressed his own practical perspective on writing
for the screen and on cinematic "art" in general (The American Mercury, 1933). Though Chandler is more sophisticated,
and more protective of the writer, it is interesting to compare his comments with Cain's as one examines "Camera
Obscura" (Raymond Chandler Speaking: "Chandler on the
Film World and Television"). Chandler too considered himself a failure as a screenwriter.

Chandler would agree with Cain when he says: "Of
the 300 or so writers actually employed in Hollywood, I sup-
pose I know fifty, and I don't know one who doesn't dislike
movie work, and wish he could afford to quit." Chandler
thought of himself as "a rather pugnacious character. I think
I proved that in Hollywood." His attitude is summed up in
his observation on "Oscar Night in Hollywood" (1949) as "the
motion picture industry's frantic desire to kiss itself on the
back of its neck."

In "Camera Obscura," Cain addresses two related
questions: 1) "Why is it that the movies seem unable to
afford the writer the requital that he finds so quickly else-

where; burning shame for work badly done; glowing pride in
work that hits the mark?" 2) "Is this really destined to be
one of the major arts, worthy of serious critical attention?"

Cain's habitual inclination to fairness obliged him to
be fair to both sides, the writer and the producer, and to
disabuse his reader of certain preconceptions about both.
"Wash out all the stories about the ghastliness of life on a
movie lot." Producers aren't beasts; there is an air of extreme courtesy and everything is done to make the writer
comfortable; and his colleagues are eager to be helpful.
Thus, the studio is like "a big club."

The critic, says Cain, "posterity's bookmaker," re-
frains from calling the movies art, because he isn't going to
make book on something so mechanical. Art "pays off on
wings, on that imaginative vitality which can fly down the
cruelly long distance through the years ... thus the critic
is concerned with what, in telegraphy, is known as the phantom circuit ... the imagination...." If it is there, who
is to be credited with it? The writer "can never be sure
that a crash of cymbals which he especially admires is not,
in reality, the sound of the conductor falling off the podium."
The high-minded writer will always be disappointed with the
movies, "will always yield place to the man in front of the
camera, who is the model, and the man behind the camera,
who is the director." Cain's conclusion balances with his
attitude as a fiction writer:

> There are worse trades than confecting entertain-
> ment, and if you realize clearly that you are at
> work on entertainment, something that lives to-
> night and tomorrow is forgotten [unlike much of
> Cain's own work, however], then the suspicion
> that you are a prostitute of the arts loses much of
> its sting.... There is good entertainment and
> bad, and a chance for plenty of honest resourceful-
> ness.... For my part, when I go to a movie, I
> am entertained best if it is unabashedly a movie,
> and not a piece of dull hoke posing as something
> else.

In the same year in which it appeared, "The Baby in
the Icebox," Cain's second story (published in The Mercury,
reprinted five times in the forties, the title story in a collection of his stories 1981), was made into a movie, She
Made Her Bed (1933) with Sally Eilers and Richard Arlen.

He had been in Hollywood, failing at writing screenplays, for two years.

In 1938, Career in C Major, written in January 1937 in twenty-eight days, was sold by the middle of February to Twentieth Century-Fox for eight thousand dollars (money that enabled Cain to go to Mexico to get background for Serenade). It appeared on the screen as Wife, Husband, Friend, with Loretta Young and Warner Baxter (the same year in which it appeared as a serial in The American Magazine as "Two Can Sing"). Everybody Does It (1949) was a popular remake of the movie, with Paul Douglas, Linda Darnell, and Celeste Holm, screenplay by Nunnally Johnson. Several of Cain's novels had their inception in story conference situations. The Root of His Evil was conceived in a luncheon conversation with Kenneth Littauer of Collier's, who wanted a modern Cinderella story. Almost ten years later, in 1938, Cain reminded Littauer of his suggestion and Cain's story outline in response to it. Sucking his pipe, Littauer said: "You know, I think that's a damned good story idea." Cain's father was dying, and during the long, grim wait, Cain dictated the story. Before Cain got back to Hollywood, James J. Geller of the William Morris office had sold the story to Universal for seventeen-thousand five-hundred dollars. The movie appeared in 1939 as When Tomorrow Comes (titled The Modern Cinderella in manuscript), with Charles Boyer and Irene Dunne. It was remade as Interlude (1957) with June Allyson and Rossano Brazzi, screenplay by Daniel Fuchs (author of the proletarian masterpiece Homage to Blenholt, 1936). It was not published as a novel until 1951, when Avon presented it under the title The Root of His Evil.

In 1940, The Embezzler was released as Money and the Woman (its Liberty serial title) with Brenda Marshall and Jeffrey Lynn. These movies offered good, solid, glittery commerical entertainment, but attracted very little critical attention, and are almost never mentioned today in film chronicles or criticism.

But adapted to the screen, some of Cain's novels were "legendary successes." In his study of movie and television censorship, The Face on the Cutting Room Floor, Murry Schumach chronicles the long struggle of movie producers with the Breen office over Double Indemnity, "a trailblazer in movie history ... the first movie in which both the male and female protagonists were thorough villians." It also paved the way for the private eye film noir of the forties.

In 1935, Metro submitted the novel itself for Breen's scrutiny; his negative report went to Paramount, Fox, Warner Brothers and Columbia as well, since all five companies were interested in the "property." Finally, a script treatment by Billy Wilder and Charles Brackett, submitted in 1943, passed the censors, mainly because the Code's restrictions had been relaxed. The presentation of adultery in Double Indemnity made victory in the battle over the same element in From Here to Eternity possible. Double Indemnity, says Schumach, was one of the most important movies to ease interpretations of the Code, to force "the watchdogs of the Code to become more aware of the considerable changes in American morals, mores and educational standards since the early thirties when the code was written" (63-70).

Double Indemnity appeared in 1943. Produced by Joseph Sistrom at Paramount, it was written for the screen by Billy Wilder and Raymond Chandler, and starred Fred MacMurray, Barbara Stanwyck, Edward G. Robinson, and Tom Powers. There is some dispute as to the extent of Wilder's authorship; his name appears first in the publication of the script in Gassner's Best Film Plays--1945. It is generally considered an artistic gem, "a landmark in the art of the cinema, in solid entertainment and everything else good that can be said of a motion picture." In his classic book on the movies, The Film Till Now, Paul Rotha called "dynamic" Double Indemnity Wilder's "most promising work to date" (1949); it shows him to be a "first-rate craftsman with a fine sense of movie melodrama." (A similar movie, he felt, was Chandler's original script, The Blue Dahlia, 1946). Wilder is a somewhat Cain-like tough guy, with "a mind full of Gillette blue blades, " says William Holden.

Double Indemnity was Raymond Chandler's first assignment (he went to work for Paramount in 1943, and quit in 1946, a career similar to, though vastly more successful than, Cain's). Cain tells of his encounter with Chandler and Wilder. Complaining that Chandler was throwing away Cain's nice, terse dialogue, Wilder got some student actors in from Paramount school, coached them, and let Chandler hear what it would be like if he would only put in the script what was in the book. It sounded like holy hell, to Wilder's utter astonishment. Then Chandler explained to Wilder what the trouble was:

> 'I could have told you, ' said Chandler, 'that Cain's dialogue, in his fiction, is written to the eye.

That ragged righthand margin that you find so exciting, is wonderful to look at, and exciting, as
you say, but it can't be recited by actors. Now
that we've got that out of the way, let's dialogue
it in the same spirit as he has in the book, but
not the identically same words. ' They got me over
there, reportedly to discuss something else, but
I detected the real reason. Wilder wanted to see
me in the hope that I would contradict Chandler,
and somehow explain what had evaporated when the
kids tried to do my lines. But at once, I bore
Chandler out--reminding Wilder I could write spo-
ken stuff well enough, but on the printed page there
just wasn't room for talky climaxes. Chandler, an
older man a bit irked by Wilder's omniscience, had
this odd little smile on his face as the talk went on
(Letter to Madden).

To Hamish Hamilton, his English publisher, Chandler
wrote: "Working with Billy Wilder on Double Indemnity was
an agonizing experience and has probably shortened my life,
but I learned from it about as much about screen writing as
I am capable of learning, which is not very much" (135), an
attitude similar to Cain's. Chandler received an academy
award nomination for the best-written screenplay for Double
Indemnity. The Maltese Falcon didn't start a trend in high-
budget pictures; Double Indemnity did. Perhaps partly for
that reason Chandler was called the best of hard-boiled writers. In a letter to his producer, Sistrom, Chandler said
that there was "no question but that Double Indemnity started it, although is was not exactly a mystery" (130).

Max Lerner devoted a few pages to the movie in his
Public Journal. He found it absorbing, a "good Hollywood
product, moving with pace, economy, credibility, and filled
with tension. " It had a minimum of prettifying and no phoney,
sickening Hollywood moralizing. He found it a better movie
than the "worthier" Wilson, because Double Indemnity does
what Hollywood does best. It has a "density" and "a dimension that juts out of the screen into American life. " Lerner
is moved to use the term "tragedy" loosely, in discussing
Wilson and Huff and Phyllis. It has often been remarked in
discussions of movie melodramas, such as the hard-boiled
ones, that, as Penelope Houston says, "the open melodrama,
from the wartime Double Indemnity, which virtually set a
cycle in motion, through Mildred Pierce, with Joan Crawford
in suffering close-up against in the night sky, to such rococo

exercises as The Strange Love of Martha Ivers, has proved
a good deal more durable than many of the movies which set
out to be significant at all costs, and ended up looking merely
laborious" (46).

James Agee had mixed feeling about the movie's achievement, but what he said about it describes quite perceptively key qualities of Cain's novels as well.

> If you laid Double Indemnity and Frenchman's Creek
> end to end you might still prefer to spend the eve-
> ning with Madame Bovary; yet you might find a few
> things mildly worth examining in these two so dif-
> ferent, so similar reflections of current attitudes
> toward bourgeois adultery.   The James Cain story
> ... is to a fair extent soaked in and shot through
> with money and the cooly intricate immorality of
> money ...   money and sex and readiness to mur-
> der are as inseparably interdependent as the Holy
> Trinity (Agee on Film, 1958, 119).

But "the picture never fully takes hold of its opportunities
...   perhaps because those opportunities ... are appreciat-
ed chiefly as surfaces and atmosphere and as very tellable
trash."   The affair "is as sexless as it is loveless," and
Stanwyck's "icy hair and teeth and dresses are well-worked
out toward communicating this idea," but Wilder didn't make
enough of "the tensions of the separateness of the lovers
after the murder or of the coldly nauseated despair and nostalgia which the murderer would feel."   Agee felt "that this
sort of genre love-scene ought to smell like the inside of an
overwrought Electrolux."   He found the movie good, gratify-
ing, though essentially cheap, "but smart and crisp and cruel
like a whole type of American film which developed softening
of the brain after the early thirties ...   The Cain story is
trash at best; at its worst it is highly respectable, set beside Daphne du Maurier's little bathroom classic, Frenchman's Creek."

Agee preferred Murder My Sweet, for "even it messi-
ness and semi-accomplishment made me feel better about it
than about the much better-finished, more nearly unimpeach-
able, but more academic and complacent Double Indemnity."
Nevertheless, he listed Double Indemnity as one of the best
of the year, exemplary of what happens when

> an intelligent director and an intelligent boss work
> smoothly together ...   it brings back into the

movies a lot of acid things, which ought to be there.
But it brings no new ones, and it does not handle
the old ones, I would say, with any notable ingenuity or interest in taking risks. Rather, it is strictly expert--a good thing of itself perhaps; but it
looks to me as if the expertness were always as
sharply controlled by what is dead sure at the box-
office as by what is right (138).

Later, Agee noted the effect of Double Indemnity upon such
movies as They Won't Believe Me (1947).

Thanks to the fact that the ice was broken with the
Wilder-Sistrom movie of James M. Cain's Double
Indemnity, Hollywood can now get by with filming
this kind of shabby 'realism.' The blessing is
mixed. Apparently, U.S. moviegoers have matured
to the point where they will stand for reasonably
frank images of unhappy marriage, sour love affairs, and of a disease so gravely epidemic as
Mr. Young's obsessive desire [in They Won't Believe Me] to stay in the money at all costs. But
in this, as in most such 'adult' movies, the semi-
maturity is well-mixed with trashiness (374).

Still later, he used Double Indemnity as a milestone: "Nobody thought they could get away with Double Indemnity, but
they did" (Agee on Film, 411).

The most fascinating, imaginative, insightful and sustained analysis of movies made from Cain's novels is found
in about forty pages of Parker Tyler's Magic and Myth of
the Movies. Tyler's conclusion on Double Indemnity is ingenious:

The lugubrious face of the movie is provided by
the fact to the Phillises and Neffs of this world
there seems available no other form of compensa-
tion for sexual inadequacy but money. Despite its
barbarously Zolaesque quality--and a little because
of it--this movie is one of the most psychologically
cogent ever to emerge from ... Hollywood--
presenting, as it does so ingeniously, the insurance
company's judgment of sexual problems. Neff's
pathological illusions is one of the diseases of American culture: that salesmanship can be an esthetic
value. The larger truth may be that, analogously

to those who adopt and cultivate a war psychology,
Neff desperately sells himself the idea of murder-
ous violence as an aid to moral enthusiasm--in his
case an enthusiasm for sex.

A recent evaluation of Double Indemnity appears in Leslie
Halliwell's The Filmgoer's Companion: "The 40s are a pretty dated era at present, but this tawdry crime story ...
still packs a punch" (235). The 1973 television remake, with
Richard Crenna, Samantha Eggar, and Lee J. Cobb, follows
the original very closely and very ineptly.

In 1945, Warner Brothers released Mildred Pierce,
with screenplay by Ranald MacDougall, starring Joan Crawford, Jack Carson, Zachary Scott, Bruce Bennett, Eve Arden,
and Ann Blyth, produced by Jerry Wald, directed by Michael
Curtiz.

Agee called "the tawdry, bitter Mildred Pierce" one of
the best of the year, and Crawford's performance her best.
It won her an academy award. It was

> a nasty, gratifying version of the James Cain novel
> about suburban grass-widowhood and the power of
> the negative passion for money and all money can
> buy. Attempt made to sell Mildred as noble when
> she is merely idiotic or at best pathetic; but con-
> stant, virulent, lambent attention to money and its
> effects, and more authentic suggestions of sex than
> one hopes to see in American films. [Veda] is as
> good an embodiment of all that is most terrifying
> about native contemporary adolescence as I ever
> hope to see .... As movies go, it is one of the
> few anywhere near honest ones, if that is of any
> importance (176).

In his Introduction to the film script of Mildred Pierce,
Albert J. LaValley points out the "most significant ways in
which the novel differs from the film": there is no murder;
Cain does not use flashbacks, the time span is longer; the
narration is not first person; Veda achieves a successful career as a coloratura; "the setting is much more tawdry and
lower class"; "the narrative is very episodic in structure with
events linked loosely, much less dramatically." Cain wrote
to producer Jerry Wald protesting those changes. "The film
departs strikingly from its source ... by tying into different cinematic traditions: the women's movie, film noir,

and murder mysteries" (10). "Cain's novels of the late
1930s and early 1940s constitute one of the fundamental influences on film noir" (13), but ironically, the "tone and style"
of the movie version of Mildred Pierce are "far removed
from Cain's novel" (10). The film moves away "from the
Warners social dramas and women's movies of the thirties
toward the dark, brooding film noir of the forties with its
stress on melodrama, the unconscious, and unsettling emotions." "Mildred's nobility has overtones of masochism"
(11). While "the noir framework and Crawford's glacial performance emphasize a guilt-ridden Mildred, capable of trickery and lies," the movie is distinguished from classic Warners noir films by a "tangle of passions and duplicitous motives and the bitter views of marriage, family, and business
...   " (12).

LaValley looks at Jerry Wald's role as producer ("it
was his decision to tell the story in flashback in the manner
of Double Indemnity"); Catherine Turney's scripts and the
comments of Albert Maltz (proletarian novelist turned scriptwriter); Margaret Gruen's ("Almost lunatic freedom") and
William Faulkner's versions ("extravagant," "lurid," "strange,"
"bizarre," "Gothic"); Ranald MacDougall's scripts and
Louise Pierson's revisions (a veteran radio writer, "with a
keen dramatic sense," MacDougall finally fused the women's
movie with film noir); director Michael Curtiz and set design-
er Anton de Grot (Europeans who created a "graceful mise-
en-scene with echoes of a European expressionist style" and
"techniques"); Crawford ("Mildred Pierce is an icon of Joan
Crawford's life"), and the rest of the cast; promotion ("Mildred Pierce--don't ever tell anyone what she did") and critical response (generally positive, especially in recent years).

In both Double Indemnity and Mildred Pierce, James
T. Farrell saw a confusion of public taste. That Cain's
novels on film end unhappily is taken as a sign that Hollywood is growing up, becoming sophisticated, turning to realism. Farrell disputes this interpretation because he feels
the films are false. Mildred Pierce opens with a murder,
though there is none in the novel. "The consequences of
the Hollywood alterations of this already Hollywoodized realism are such that the film becomes stupid and senseless" (88).
Farrell makes the same charges against Double Indemnity.
Having gotten by the production code, its realism and sophistication are "enhanced and made vivid by the familiar and
glamorous background of sin in our times" (88-89). The

magic of the movies capitalizes on a glamor that goes to
create a pseudorealism.

In From Reverence to Rape, The Treatment of Women
in the Movies (1974), Molly Haskell provides a feminist perspective on Mildred Pierce and Double Indemnity. "Crawford
took the guts out of the character.... The obsession with
the daughter (Ann Blyth), with its erotic implications... is a
veiled expression of self-love, and takes on the aspect of nar-
cissism that is the ultimate Crawford posture" (179). Eve
Arden's inflated role proves to be, from the feminist angle,
both more admirable and finally more perverse. In Double
Indemnity, Stanwyck's attraction to MacMurray "is geniunely
sexual, or sexual-homicidal (sex being the equivalent of evil,
evil the metaphor for sex)" (197). Both movies are "verile
and existentially skeptical" (207).

Many critics, Wilson and Lerner, particularly, early
predicted that The Postman Always Rings Twice could not be
filmed. But an expertly mechanized, slick movie of hard
surfaces, in some scenes a literal transcription of the
novel, excluding the sex scenes, appeared in 1946, produced by MGM, written by Harry Ruskin and Nevin
Busch (whose novel Duel in the Sun somewhat resembles
The Postman). Not much has been written about this
movie, though I found it as memorable as the first two.
Agee termed it "mainly a terrible misfortune from start
to finish."

In Running Away From Myself, A Dream Portrait of
America Drawn from the Films of the 40's, Barbara Deming
reads like a cross between Parker Tyler and Pauline Kael
as she analyzes The Postman, Double Indemnity, and Duel
in the Sun in a chapter called "Maybe I Know a Way to Get
Clear of the Mess!" (The Nihilists). "These heroes ...
go asking for trouble," she says. They make a "death-seek
ing gesture." What she says of Double Indemnity describes
most of Cain's novels and their movie versions. "From the
very start ... we move with the" lovers "toward a known
fatality," and "the thrill the moment actually holds for us is
the thrill of the possibility that they may both be destroyed."
Murder has become an "irrelevance." We move swiftly
with the lovers in the quest of a promise or wish, "a breath-
less intent walk" into a "vivifying death." The Postman and
Double Indemnity "light up" other films for us (172, 179-80).

For Pauline Kael, The Postman is "a shoddy melodrama" about "animals-in-love," "a fair example of movies

as products ...

> I must admit that I've never really understood the
> logic or appeal of these postman-fate-retribution
> systems in which one escapes the crimes one has
> committed, but is trapped by accidents in which one
> is innocent; but just as surely as tragic fate is
> Greek, this cheap little ironic twist is American
> (Kiss Kiss Bang Bang, 333).

In Screening the Novel (1980), Gabriel Miller devotes
twenty pages to a comparison of the novel with the movie
version of The Postman Always Rings Twice (the book is odd-
ly subtitled "Rediscovered American Fiction in Film"; neither
the novel nor the movie needs rediscovering, do they?) He
concludes that

> the film version ... is only intermittently relat-
> ed to Cain's vision and remains consistently uncer-
> tain of its own logic; ultimately it betrays all its
> assets of casting and story in a disastrous attempt
> to reconcile an existential drama with the world of
> reason and hope which it inherently denies (63).

By contrast, the 1981 version starring Jack Nicholson
and Jessica Lange, directed by Bob Rafelson, script by the
young playwright David Mamet, may appear at first glance a
more faithful adaptation of Cain's characters, incidents, and
vision than the 1946 version, but its exaggerated homage in
color to film noir atmospherics and its pseudoanimal sexuality
are only overreaching attempts to do in the eighties what
Hollywood was forbidden to do in the forties; its simple-minded
realism undercuts the fable quality so essential to Cain's
vision and effect, a quality that the Garfield-Turner version,
whatever its faults, did convey. For instance, Garfield's
first look at Turner, a classic cinematic gimmick not articulated in the novel, is more faithful to Cain's "vision" than
Nicholson's first look at Lange, which has all the electric
impact, in cinematic terms, of watching paint dry on a court-
house wall. Nicholson's qualities as an actor--arrogance,
intelligence, wit--conflict too often with Frank's qualities as a
character. Whatever one might claim as the virtues of this
space-age version, the absence of Cain's famous pace defuses
their effect.

In her review of the 1981 movie version of The Postman, Pauline Kael declares that not only does it lunge at high

art and fall on its face, it is unfaithful to the novel.

> This picture isn't a cloddish disgrace; you can see
> the taste and craftsmanship that have gone into it.
> It's overcontrolled, though, and methodical in its
> pacing. It's wrongheaded.... With all that ele-
> gant cinematography, the film has no images that
> stay in the mind the way Cain's descriptions do
> .... Rafelson and Mamet don't seem to know a
> good story when it's right in their hands, so they
> cheapen it.... The moviemakers use Cain's story
> to carry meanings that are far less gallant than
> his.... The movie seems twice the length of the
> novel, yet it never gets the point (The New Yorker,
> 160-66).

Roger Manvell in New Cinema in Europe saw greater
significance in the Italian version. After continual interfer-
ence, Luchino Visconti's Ossessione (1942) was passed by
Mussolini himself. "It was like a bomb exploding in the cinema," Visconti said. "People saw a film which they had
not thought possible" (18). The film was so realistic that
it ran into further censorship problems in Italy. Manvell
would agree with Arthur Knight's claim that it was "a true
masterpiece that contained all the seeds of the postwar neo-
realist movement" (The Liveliest Art, 222). Manvell's description of its concerns make it sound like a proletarian novel
of the thirties: "the deep attachment to the vitality of working-
class life, the uncompromising photography of Italian
streets and highways ... and the determination to show how
poverty, over-crowding and sordid living conditions affect the
humanity of men" (18). The American version had no effect
at all on movies anywhere; the American slant on Cain had
already made its international impact in Double Indemnity.
Visconti flagrantly violated copyright laws and for many years
MGM refused to allow prints of the movie to enter the U.S.
There was also a French version, Le Dernier Tournant
(1939).

Among other movies made from Cain novels was an
incredibly mutilated, bad adaptation of Serenade in 1955, with
Mario Lanza and Joan Fontaine, screenplay by Ivan Goff, Ben
Roberts, and John Twist. Serenade is under option. Love's
Lovely Counterfeit, the only novel Cain wrote with a movie
sale in mind, appeared in 1956 as Slightly Scarlet, with
Rhonda Fleming, Arlene Dahl, and John Payne, screenplay by
Robert Blees, produced by Filmcrest. In 1965, Past All Dis-

honor was bought by Tom Mankowiecz to star Robert Wagner,
but that deal fell through. In 1981, Peter Bogdanovich acquired the rights. Galatea is under option.

As of August 25, 1981, H. N. Swanson, Cain's Hollywood agent since the early thirties, had received more calls
about Cain and his material over the summer "than almost
any client that we ever represented, which included: Raymond
Chandler, John O'Hara, Ernest Hemingway, and William Faulkner" (Letter to Madden). The Butterfly has been filmed,
with Stacy Keach and Orson Welles, the locale shifted from
the coal mines of West Virginia to the silver mines of Nevada
--proving that Hollywood madness is not a lamentable phenomenon of the forties and fifties. None of Cain's eleven novels
written after 1942 have been adapted to the screen.

Cain said in 1946 that he knew while he was writing
them that his novels would have censor trouble,

> yet I never toned one of them down, or made the
> least change to court the studio's favor. In Past
> All Dishonor, for at least four versions, the girl
> was not of the oldest profession; she was the neice
> of the lady who ran the brothel, and for four ver-
> sions the story laid an egg. I then had to admit
> to myself that it had point only when she was a
> straight piece of trade goods. Putting the red light
> over the door, I knew, would cost me a picture
> sale, and so far it has; it is in there just the same,
> and it made all the difference in the world with the
> book (Preface, Butterfly).

As for the effect of the movies, Edmund Wilson sees dark
implications in the fact that, as Cain states on the jacket, the
idea for writing the book came on a trip to Virginia City "in
connection with a picture." Wilson sees in the novel

> a lot of old studio properties: guns, saloons, gamb-
> ling wheels, Wells Fargo, silver bonanzas, gallop-
> ing horses, the bad woman of magnificent insolence
> who keeps the boys shooting it out for her favors.
> It used to be said about Cain's earlier novels that
> they sounded like movie scripts too outrageous to
> be produced.

By 1946, Wilson felt that Cain had "been eaten alive by
the movies" (The New Yorker, 90).

The earlier comments of Wilson and Farrell on the movie elements in Cain sum up the typical charges. As we follow the development of Cain's plots, Wilson says, "we find ourselves more and more disconcerted at knocking up--to the destruction of illusion--against the blank and hard planes and angles of something we know all too well: the wooden old conventions of Hollywood." Wilson calls these novels, produced in Cain's time off from the movies, "a Devil's parody of the movies ... Mr. Cain is the ame damnee of Hollywood. All the things that have been excluded by the Catholic censorship: sex, debauchery, unpunished crime, sacrilege against the Church--Mr. Cain has let them loose in these stories with a gusto as of pent-up ferocity that the reader cannot but share" ("Boys," 21-22).

Farrell felt that the movies defeated a great talent in Cain.

> Cain is between the serious and tragic work by men like Dreiser and the popular writers. A master at playing between both sides ... he is a literary thrill-producer who profits by the reaction against the sentimentality of the other years and, at the same time, gains from the prestige of more serious and exploratory writing. Thus James M. Cain is not an insignificant or unimportant American literary phenomenon. He has helped to perfect a form which can properly be termed movietone realism (85).

Though Mildred Pierce has the appearance of greater reality than the movies project, he squandered his opportunity by developing that novel "in terms of Hollywood simplicities." Cain's novels at best are "literary movies." Even the more sympathetic Lerner feels that too much of Cain's writing depends, like popular movies, on terrific pace, shock, and formula writing. I believe that even in his least artistic novels, Cain writes high quality tough movie dialogue, such as the best of Frank Fenton, Philip Yordan, and Robert Riskin. Ironically, the novelistic dialogue of Cain the failed scriptwriter has had a tremendous effect, through his novels, on successful movie writers.

Aware of the realities of the cinema, as he experienced them, Cain knew that what he had to say could be said only in the solitude of novel writing, only in the way a novel can say things. Chandler felt the same way. "The challenge of screenwriting," Chandler said, "is to say much in little and then take half of that little out and still preserve an ef-

fect of leisure and natural movement," a good definition of
tough novels, as well, going all the way back to The Black
Mask school. But "such a technique requires experiment and
elimination" which the conditions of moviemaking deny the
writer himself (Raymond Chandler Speaking, 119).

Ann Blyth, Zachary Scott and Joan Crawford in Mildred
Pierce (1945).

CHAPTER FOUR

Cain and the "Pure" Novel

Among writers, critics, and other serious readers, James M. Cain has an unusual reputation for a so-called popular writer. This reputation is based on The Postman Always Rings Twice (1934), Serenade (1937), and The Butterfly (1947); some would also rank Mildred Pierce (1941) and Double Indemnity (1944) with Cain's best. Little has been written about Cain, but the fact that he should have been discussed as he has been suggests that his novels are more important in American literature than some readers have supposed.

Critics first write Cain off as a popular novelist and then proceed to reproach him for failing to rise to the level of artistic achievement toward which they have felt he is striving. Max Lerner believes that Cain, "novelist-laureate of the crime of passion in America," takes his task seriously, but "phony tensions" defeat him. Wilbur M. Frohock admits that Cain is "sure-handed" with his materials but charges that his technique is "fraudulent." James T. Farrell and Edmund Wilson are convinced that Cain's special technique and style defeat his often promising though seldom lucidly conceived thematic purposes. His characters have been called crude, amoral, and uncomplicated, while being compared with characters like Camus' Meursault. He has been accused of writing by formula and adhering to a technique that is basically "movie-tone realism." William Rose Benet has called his style the best of the hard-boiled school, having "a fast rhythm that is art." Edmund Wilson, commenting on The Postman Always Rings Twice, suggests the general critical attitude: "Brilliant moments of insight redeemed the unconscious burlesque; and there is enough of the real poet in Cain--both in writing and in imagination--to make one hope for something better" ("Boys," 22).

While W. M. Frohock and other historians of American literature deplore his exploitation of sex and violence, few

61

fail to note Cain's influence. Cain has influenced those writers who have created the shallower parts in the stream of
American, and perhaps French, fiction, but he has also influenced Albert Camus.

Cain himself suggests the kind of question that perhaps needs to be asked about his work. "I don't lack for at
least as much recognition as I deserve" (Butterfly, xii).
Looking at him in his own field of vision and in the light of
his best work, how much recognition does James M. Cain
deserve? With that question, embracing the whole tough-guy
school, critics have reopened an important chapter in American literature.

In the "pure novel" tradition of Flaubert and Gide,
Joseph Hergesheimer aspired to "write a novel as compact
and deadly as an automatic," and Georges Simenon has said,
"I want to carve my novel in a piece of wood." Cain has--
twice: The Postman and The Butterfly. Narrative, action,
rhythm, character, and style, unencumbered by philosophy,
are primary elements in a novel which, generated by pace,
should move in a brief exposure toward the pure condition
of abstract art and unprogrammatic music. Neither an instrument of instruction nor a medium of information, the
pure novel is concerned only with its own drama.

In his best books Cain seems to have written what
Georges Simenon, discussing his own work, has sketchily
described as the "pure" novel. Cain has a story to tell,
always about a man and a woman, and all his creative energy
is directed toward getting the story told as briefly and forcibly as possible. Of his own work, Simenon has said:

> And the beginning will always be the same; it is
> almost a geometrical question: I have such a man,
> such a woman, in such surroundings. What can
> happen to them to oblige them to go to their limits?
> That's the question. It will be sometimes a very
> simple incident, anything which will change their
> lives (Cowley, Writers at Work, 151).

Simenon, also a popular writer, considers himself a creator,
not a moralist like Gide, the serious writer who had great
respect for him. While the novelist, by the very nature of
his medium, cannot entirely escape making moral and social
value judgments, writers in one tradition have tried since the
time of Flaubert (as poets have tried since the time of Valery)

to make a novel (a poem) as "pure" a work of art as a stat-
ue is. In Rodin's art, one has subject and treatment, but
form and space provide the most exciting elements in the experience. The "pure" novel, Simenon says,

> will do only what the novel can do. I mean that it
> doesn't have to do any teaching or any work of jour-
> nalism. In a pure novel you wouldn't take sixty
> pages ... to describe the South of Arizona....
> Just the drama with only what is absolutely part of
> this drama. What I think about novels today is
> almost a translation of the rules of tragedy into
> the novel. I think the novel is the tragedy of our
> day (Writers, 156).

Reminding one of Poe's dictum regarding poetry, Simenon
believes that the novel, like tragedy, should be short enough
to enable a reader to absorb it in one sitting.

Cain's comments about his own work reveal a serious
concern with the craft of fiction and a clear understanding of
his intentions in so far as I have been able to discern them.

Of his "literary ideals and methods of composition,"
Cain states that because he always had difficulties with technique, he delayed writing for ten years. Like Henry James,
notes Hamilton Basso, sarcastically, Cain is a writer of prefaces (for three of the first six novels). Many critics and
reviewers quote from Cain's prefaces, out of sheer delight,
though sometimes with intent to ridicule. His plays and his
short stories had little success. Suspicious of technique, he
felt that it would eventually become formula and "hoke."
Good writing was "gestative rather than fabricative." Until
he met Vincent Lawrence, he believed that writing needed only
to mirror life and to be true. Other early influences on
Cain's writing were Philip Goodman, New York theatrical
producer, H. L. Mencken, with whom Cain worked on The
Baltimore Sun, and Arthur Conan Doyle, whom he never met.
For Cain, Alice in Wonderland is the "greatest novel in the
English language" (Paris Review, 123). As a writer of movie
scripts and plays, Lawrence had become almost legendary by
laying down certain cinematic principles. His banner was:
technique.

Cain's credo is that narrative and action, not philosophy, are the most important qualities of a novel. When he
states that he "proposed to be true" to his "ideal of truth,"

he does not refer to meaning. Action, narrative, character, style, and other fictive elements should effect one clean, simple thrust; the novel should raise and answer its own necessary questions and refer to nothing outside itself. Like a piece of music, it should be an experience that has rhythm, style, movement, pattern, motif--an experience generated by time or pace, to use a term from drama. As with sculpture, you would feel it, see it, touch it, and there would be a sense of taste and smell, as there is when one looks at a rough Rodin, and it would be all of a piece, to be looked at from various angles, but dependent as little as possible upon anything beyond the bounds of its own immediacy.

From Vincent Lawrence, Cain got the principle of "the love-rack." It was once a rather new idea to Cain that the reader has first to care about the two main characters--to care that they are on the love-rack, to sympathize with them. So Cain made the love-rack the whole novel, not just a scene or two. "I wanted to know why every episode in the story couldn't be invented and moulded and written with a view to its effect on the love story" (Butterfly, xii). We view the lovers only in terms of the experience, which raises and answers its own questions and refers to nothing extraneous.

Murder is the best love-rack. "But in the end they would get away with it, and then what? They would find ... that the earth is not big enough for two persons who share such a dreadful secret, and eventually turn on each other" (xii). The main idea is not that the secret is dreadful, but that two lovers share it in such a way as to turn against each other. "I, so far as I can sense the pattern of my mind, write of the wish that comes true, for some reason a terrifying concept, at least to my imagination" (Butterfly, x). Cain feels this terror, then feels it with his two main characters, then makes the reader feel it, and every device of the novel that will heighten the experience is made to work.

Critics lauded Cain for the technical brilliance of The Postman's first scene. After that love scene, he "strove for a rising coefficient of intensity," hoping to hit real passion and to give a full rendition of his father's definition of tragedy: "force of circumstance driving the protagonist to the commission of a dreadful act" (xii). Cain's father was President of Washington College in Maryland. Because of early fiascoes, Cain "acquired ... such a morbid fear of boring a reader that I certainly got the

habit"--and developed the technique--"of needling a story at
the least hint of a letdown" (xv). Lerner says that Cain's
general theme is one "of love and death coiled up with each
other like fatal serpents. It is love-in-death-and-rebirth-in
love" ("Cain in the Movies," 47). Although not all the novels
are about murder, all do use the concept of the love-rack:
"all concern some high adventure on which a man and a woman embark" (Butterfly, xii). Only in Career in C Major is that
adventure a comic one. Cain once felt there weren't enough "nat-
urals" for this type of story. He often missed passion and
hit lust, which is "neither interesting nor pretty." In 1942,
he said, "I want to tell tales of a little wider implication
than those which deal exclusively with one man's relation to
one woman. In the future, what was valid in the technical
organization of my first few novels will be synthesized, I
hope, into a somewhat larger technique" (Butterfly, xv).

Whatever he meant by "larger technique," his finest
are those lean novels in which everything is cut down to the
essentials.

Tough optimism is clearly expressed in all of Cain's
writing. At times he is cynical and satirical, but the American brand of masculine romanticism is also active, and occasionally even sentimentality intrudes. In Cain's world,
change, luck, coincidence, gamble and counter-gamble, risk,
audacity, and the ability to improvise upon the given serve
his characters, but usually end in defeating them. While he
is capable of creating finely drawn moral dilemmas, as in
Mignon, he is primarily interested in the action produced by
them and their impact on character rather than in elaborat-
ing upon facets of the abstract issues.

But Cain is not all melodrama and disaster. Some
of his novels, Career in C Major, for instance, are come-
dies, and none is without humor, wit, and even lyricism.
Music is at the heart of three and is an element in most of
the other novels. Cain's mother was a fine opera singer,
Cain himself worked hard at a singing career but gave it up
for lack of talent; he continued to study music as an avocation
much of his life. His last wife, who died in 1966, was the
former Florence Macbeth of the Chicago Opera.

Of all his novels, Cain thinks The Butterfly comes
closest to art. I agree, but since The Postman Always Rings
Twice is probably more familiar, we might look at its qualifications for being the kind of "pure" novel previously sug-

gested. Except for The Moth, Mildred Pierce, and one or
two others, the novels are clearly constructed. The hero
usually meets the woman in the first few paragraphs. The
whole problem is set in the first chapter, and transitions
and turning points are swiftly executed, but seldom in a way
discordant with the rest of the book. Exposition is superflu-
ous when expedition is the ruling force. In The Postman,
Frank Chambers, a young wanderer, gets kicked off a truck
at Twin Oaks Tavern, "a roadside sandwich joint, like a million others in California" (1978 Vintage paperback edition,
p. 1). Nick, the Greek proprietor, offers him a job, but
he doesn't take it until he sees "her," Nick's wife. "Except
for the shape, she really wasn't any raving beauty, but she
had a sulky look to her, and her lips stuck out in a way that
made me want to mash them for her" (2). By page 14, they
have made love and she has suggested that they kill Nick.
The rest of the story (or more appropriately, the experience)
follows the pattern Cain and Simenon outline above. Cain
lets it "secrete its own adrenalin." In this pure novel,
Cain's deliberate intentions go no further than the immediate
experience, brief as a movie is, as unified in its impressions
as a poem usually is. Though Frank writes his story on the
eve of his execution, Cain does not even suggest the simplest
moral: crime does not pay. An intense experience, which
a man tells in such a way as to make it, briefly, our experience, it is its own reason for being.

      To the kind of novel that Cain writes, Farrell's judg-
ment that Cain's characters' values are crude has little relevance. While they apparently got their crude values from
the society that produced them, Cain does not deal with the
question of blame. His characters, clinging dogmatically to
a fragmentary set of values, plunge into situations in which
they sink as their own punishers. That they are punished
may reflect Cain's own moral attitude, or be a concession
to that of his audience, but more important is the fact that
a violent death is appropriately the culmination of all other
ingredients in Cain's "pure" novels. Cain implies that a
man deserves the lot he has. Whether he stays with it or
tries to rise above it, he is responsible. This is a hard-
boiled attitude, but Cain often declared, "I belong to no
school, hard-boiled or otherwise" (Butterfly, ix).

      The dialectics of self-deception in which Cain's
characters become ensnarled are often only potentially pro-

found; he is primarily a master of manipulation of surface action; the captive reader forgets that the characters--beyond the stark tensions of their predicament--are often not fully drawn.

Frohock claims that Cain's "valueless" characters are uncomplicated. While this is simply not true, Frank the hero in The Postman does give the impression of simplicity, although his ambivalent attitude toward people reveals a little more complexity than one may find in most 1934 murder novels: Frank can like Nick, yet kill him cold-bloodedly, and can love Cora, yet rat on her. If he were really complicated, he wouldn't be Frank Chambers, and the book is about a simple man who passes rapidly from motive to act. The situation, too, is simple, but the character relationships and the emotive concept of the novel have a depth and often a subtle complexity almost sufficient in themselves to make the novel a work of art in its special way. Give Frank fuller dimension and the concept is ruined. The novel does exactly, with very little waste or excess, what it sets out to do.

"In a Cain novel," says Frohock, "it is clear that Cain's opponent is his reader; he feints us into position and hits us before we can get our feet untangled" (Novel of Violence, 89).

This technical feat enables him to capture the reader and involve him in a kind of behavior, Frohock believes, that makes The Postman an immoral book: "We have been tricked into taking the position of potential accomplices," because we want Frank and Cora to escape. Other critics have declared that despite the excitement he generates, Cain leaves one with a sense of emptiness rather than enrichment because "the formula" defeats him (98). It does, if Cain is aiming for more than can be artistically achieved within the compass of "the formula" (a misleading term when referring to the "pure" novel).

If one must harp on the problem of meaning, Frohock's objection to Frank Chambers' lack of tragic stature must be discussed. Unendowed with any moral significance, Cain's violence merely exploits "the sensibility which informs the serious novel of violence," says Frohock (99). Although Frank Chambers is like Meursault, Cain's work lacks the large philosophical view that Camus' has. Whereas Meursault begins to experience self-knowledge in his death cell, Frank goes to his death more deluded than ever, but it does not follow that the reader shares the delusion.

It is most pertinent to look at Cain's technical devices, for he is a conscious technician of the "pure" novel. Cain discovered that the first person narrative in the Southern California argot suited his novels best. A native of Maryland whose early stories and plays were in dialect, Cain retains a certain Southern tone, pattern of speech and diction at times which leaven the coarseness of the speech he cultivates. Conscious as he is of style, he makes no conscious effort to be tough; he simply writes as he thinks the hero would speak. "In general, my style is rural rather than urban; my ear seems to like fields better than streets. I am glad of this, for I think language loses a bit of its bounce the moment its heels touch concrete" (Three, viii-ix). The first-person narrative, most effective in Postman, Serenade, and Butterfly, is made immediate by the fact that the character often writes his story as a kind of confession. Even in Cain's essays, an aggressive, almost arrogant, but commanding "I" is in control. The first person works best for his deliberate tranformation of the clichés of everyday speech. "Many of life's most moving things are banal ... I try, in using a cliché, to set it up so perhaps it gains its own awkward, pathetic eloquence" (Letter). The third person often lures Cain into literary clichés, as in his short stories for Liberty in the thirties, in Mildred Pierce, Love's Lovely Counterfeit (1942), Sinful Woman (1955), and The Magician's Wife (1965). For Joyce Carol Oates, the main flaw in Mildred Pierce, "overlong and shapeless," is its "third-person omniscient narration, which takes us too far from the victim and allows us more freedom than we want. To be successful, such narrowly-conceived art must blot out what landscape it cannot cover; hence the blurred surrealist backgrounds of the successful Cain novels, Postman ... and Serenade" ("Man Under Sentence of Death," 112).

Since Mildred Pierce is full of clichés, it is necessary to point out that it is not the clichés which spoil the style and retard the pace. The trite expressions are appropriate to Mildred's world. Cain makes conscious expressive use of

the cliché, much in the way that Wright Morris does, though
without his especial success. The focus is always on Mildred,
but had Cain allowed her to tell the story, one would have been
able to observe his ability to render action in a woman's
voice; in The Root of His Evil (1954), Carrie, who reminds
one both of Mildred and of her daughter Veda, tells her own
story, but it lacks the urgency and verisimilitude that Mildred
Pierce has. It is Cain's language that generates much of the
excitement in the explosive character relationships, presented in incendiary situations.

Cain develops a theatrical and cinematic pace that is
phenomenal in his best work. "You may not like Serenade, "
said William Rose Benet, "but I defy you to lay it down. "
Though the neat phrases sometimes falter into embarrassing
cuteness, Cain manages to infuse virtually every moment with
apparent urgency. As his simple dialogue progresses from
point to point, it sustains subtle undercurrents. While stock
devices sometimes mar his work, they are often used effectively as absurd helps or hindrances to the character who
strives to score against "the way things are. " Cain's dialogue is deceptively simple, but it performs many functions:
it foreshadows, suggests thoughts, emotions and motives.
So much happens in the swiftly paced dialogue that the reader must catch allusions and sense meaning under the dialogue,
as in the best of Hemingway. "I care almost nothing for what
my characters look like," says Cain, "being almost exclusively
concerned with their insides" (Three, xiv). The always brisk
and terrific pace, in itself a vital element in the lives of the
characters, is not impeded by unnecessary description. When
he does describe a character, as he seems compelled to do
in a third-person novel, he obviously doesn't care. Most of
his heroes are six feet tall (resembling Cain's own physique)
and have blond curly hair. Women's faces are less vivid
than their figures because faces of women, he believes, are
masks, "but their bodies, the way they walk, sit, hold their
heads, gesticulate, and eat, betray them." (Three, xiv).

When Cain uses symbolism, it is elemental, appealing
to what is basic in us; I am also convinced that it is unconscious. It is crude though appropriate to liken Cora to a

snake, to a cougar, and to the great-grandmother of all whores; it works because it does not take us away from but fastens us more firmly upon the subject. The complex pattern of motif, too, is spontaneous, as in the lyrics of folk songs.

The simplicity of Cain's style has evoked comparison with Hemingway. "Just what it is I am supposed to have got from him I have never quite made out, though I am sure it can hardly be in the realm of content, for it would be hard to imagine two men in this respect more dissimilar" (Butterfly, x). He had published a great deal of tough-style nonfiction before Hemingway ever appeared on the scene. Regarding the charge of imitation, he concludes, "It does strike me as a very odd notion that in setting out to make it good I would do the one thing certain to make it bad" (Butterfly, xiii). Cain's style is less like Hemingway's than the general aura of his books is like that of Faulkner's, in their elements of horror, despair, terror, and grotesquerie. However, he is like Hemingway in the sense that it is in his style that one gets a feeling of his sensibility. As regards the "pure" novel, he has more affinities with Flaubert than with Hemingway or Faulkner.

In the field of the novel one might add, tentatively, since it is relatively rare, the "pure" to Stephen Dedalus' three forms of art: lyrical, epical, and dramatic. "Pure" might have much the same kind of meaning for the novel that "nonobjective" has for painting. It is absurd to bring Joyce, Aquinas, and Flaubert into a discussion of the special quality of Cain's best novels only if one insists on overemphasizing the problem of meaning in them. The serious reader returns to The Postman not for its meaning, or even its characters, but to experience again an aesthetic emotion. He regards thought and content as seriously as he would if he were looking at a loaded gun on a table; subtle, complex contemplation is almost no part of the experience.

"That is beautiful the apprehension of which pleases," said Aquinas. Necessary for aesthetic stasis are wholeness, harmony, and radiance. It is possible for a novel to possess any of these qualities to the extent that the plastic arts--and also those forms devoid of apparent subject matter, music and architecture--do? Flaubert wanted in literature the same impersonality one attributes to Greek sculpture. "The illusion ... arises ... from the impersonality of the work. It is one of my principles that one must not write oneself in. The artist must stand to his work as God to his creation, invisible and all powerful; he must be everywhere felt but nowhere seen" (Novels in the Making, ed. Buckler, 69).

Cain's seeming lack of personal involvement in moral and other such considerations enables him to achieve this impersonality, and in surrendering himself, he conquers his art. It is in the area of form and technique that Cain deserves study, since his novels take us in the direction of "pure" form and technique. Some may say that in reading Cain one has a kinetic ("impure"), rather than an aesthetic experience, causing one to feel desire or loathing, depending on one's moral attitudes. But Cain's characters, themes, and situations are apparently so simple and exaggerated--although on closer scrutiny they have a special kind of complexity--that one must simply exercise a "willing suspension of disbelief for aesthetic remuneration.

My intention here is not to formulate criteria for the "pure" novel. The form has intriguing possibilities, and I merely wish to indicate that one may begin a study with Cain. Some qualifications pertaining to the more relevant elements --style, technique, and form--have been discussed.

Cain's main subjects are sex and money, major elements in the lives of a great many people. Money is sometimes a substitute for sex, a source of sublimated power, but when sex comes into play again, it becomes the motive force, and the precipice is not far away. For sex and money, the lovers, principally the male, lose themselves in an audacious endeavor. A strange aura of evil, and sometimes of pagan-Christian religion as well, surrounds that endeavor; a kind of religious motive, mixed up with sex or love, is behind the compulsion to confess. Outside society and its morality, the lovers respond to a mystique of their own, requiring purification and rebirth, and sometimes redemption or atonement through deeds or death, if the sex is to continue and the money to be enjoyed. The sex may require the money, but the pursuit of money frustrates the pursuit of sex, or vice versa. Sex here is animalistic, lacking the niceties of conventional romance, although the male may have a romantic attitude toward life, encouraged by the realistic woman either to facilitate her ensnarement of him or to keep him. The male often becomes aware of a strain of cowardice or unmanliness in himself.

This is the simple pattern of Cain's "pure" novels.

When the thematic and narrative pattern, the characters, and
the technique become complicated, as in The Moth, the results are an ordinary novel with flashes of Cain genius. The
Moth, an obvious attempt at a serious theme, flits about too
much; the concept holds up, but the details weigh it down,
and it is too long, a failure of style and technique on the
whole, though not in all its parts. Cain's longest book, somewhat autobiographical in the early section, this novel is almost
picaresque, covering many years, a multiplicity of characters,
much territory, many episodes, and much of the manners of
all classes. Most of Cain's novels are concerned with a few
characters over a short period of time in one locale; only
two are set in the historical past. His style and technique
function best when his theme, his character relationships,
and his milieu are simple.

        Cain's world is a man's world, normally viewed
through the eyes of the male. Although the narrator usually
writes down his story, he sounds as though he were telling
it. The confessional device is used when the story ends unhappily, to use a movie term. Each hero has a different but
simple motive for confessing. From the first novel through
the last, motive undergoes an interesting evolution.

        Frank Chambers writes his story in his death cell,
not because he wants his fellow man to have a better opinion
of him, but because he has a romantic notion that if the world
knows he loves Cora, that knowledge will lend a purity to
their love. Like Meursault, he wants society to witness his
death, his innocence, and his love; unlike Meursault, he desires prayers for himself and Cora, but he doesn't ask forgiveness for killing Nick and taking his wife. Frank and
Cora, by their natures and the nature of their relationship,
are "outsiders"; his confession has purely selfish motives,
as do Walter Huff's in Double Indemnity and Howard Sharpe's
in Serenade. But the motives in Past All Dishonor (1946),
The Butterfly, and Galatea (1953) are almost purely social--
to help other men avoid the same fate as the confessor. In
The Moth Jack Dillon writes to please his father; even in
Cain's short stories one discovers the compulsion to confess
or the social-purpose motive for first-person narrative.
Edmund Wilson early sensed a rudimentary social awareness
in Cain himself. In The Moth (1948), this awareness is quite
apparent, especially in the treatment of conditions during the
Depression and of the problem of social responsibility. But
in his most effective work, Cain is interested less in the
criminal's relation to society than in his relation to himself

or himself and his lover, relations with a greater immediacy.

Bemused by violence, Americans like to feel out, Cain
says, all the nuances of the cliché "There but for the grace
of God go I." To involve the reader more intimately in the
social communion with violence, ritualized by mass media reportage, Cain deals with characters just removed from the
gangster and private eye milieu. The death of a man like
Frank releases the reader from the guilt of having identified
with the character's wishes. Cain claims that "the world's
great literature is populated by thorough-going heels." Most
of his own novels describe "life among the heels and the har-
pies." Though doomed by his faults, none whines about his
punishment; on the eve of his execution, Frank Chambers refuses to shift responsibility for his actions to a hostile society. Cain admires the clear, hard, cold mind, and thrusts
his characters into actions in which their daring and know-how
enable them to meet any challenge. His typical hero is an
"educated roughneck": a meat-packing executive, an insurance
agent, a bank executive, an engineer. But even his boxers,
farmers, and mechanics prove adroit. These men crave
praise and are sometimes immobilized, momentarily, by
condemnation. But Cain's men aren't afraid to be afraid;
they weep or vomit when the sex is out of reach or the violence goes wrong. In "Tribute to a Hero," an early essay
for The Mercury, he recalls a reluctant football hero at
Washington College, where Cain's father was president. The
boy displayed a combination of guts and cowardice that is seen
in most Cain heroes and becomes a dangerous effeminacy in
in Howard Sharp, the hard-boiled opera singer of Serenade.

One aspect of self-dramatization is the inside-dopester
strain in American character. Many American writers, Hemingway, for instance, strive to speak with authority on the
fine points of special subjects. As a former journalist, Cain
exhibits in his novels this voraciousness for facts, and there-
in lies part of his appeal. With the audacity and bravura of
the fact-armed amateur, the Cain hero triumphs over great
obstacles (though only momentarily, for when the wish comes
true, nothing helps--he falls off the end of the plank). In
the historical novels especially--Past All Dishonor and Mignon
(1963)--Cain's immersion in his minutely researched background causes a conflict of intention: historical accuracy is
achieved at the expense of drama. But if The Moth and The
Institute (1976) collapse under a burden of inside dope, The
Butterfly succeeds, though all three were heavily researched
on the scene (he worked as a coal miner in West Virginia)
and in the record.

In all Cain's tough heroes there is a streak of something unmanly of physical, sometimes moral, cowardice.
In Serenade, Cain treats Howard Sharp's homosexual tendency and Juana's suspicion of it with such subtlety that it contributes partly to the book's suspense.   Sharpe is afraid to
discover the horrible thing Juana sees in him, and Walter
Huff in Double Indemnity is afraid of Phyllis, a psychotic in
love with death, toward whom he feels drawn.   "I kept telling myself to get out of there, and get quick, and never come
back. But ... what I was doing was peeping over that edge,
and all the time I was trying to pull away from it, there was
something in me that kept edging a little closer, trying to
get a better look" (18).

Whether for love or money, but usually for both,
Cain's heroes are always leaning over the precipice for a
better look at "the wish. "   Part of Cain's concept of a real
man is this inner struggle with fear that gives off enough heat to
propel him through various adventures.   Always he gets the
woman and he gets the money, or whatever he is after, but
when he does, he falls over the precipice, clutching both.

Cain's tough heroes are romantics who see life as one
fierce adventure, who plunge into every situation heedless of
realities.   Frank is a simple-minded Whitman whose weakness
is his desire for a woman in his arms on the open road.

> "Just you and me and the road, Cora. "
> "Just you and me and the road. "
> "Just a couple of tramps. "
> "Just a couple of gypsies, but we'll be together" (27).

Jack Dillon's weakness is romanticism, symbolized by a green
luna moth, and lived out in an almost lifelong flight from an
impossible childhood love.

Cain's women are often stronger than his men, who
often cry with joy and despair.   It is as though Cain were
trying to portray the American male fully and fascinatingly
by showing that he has an effeminate streak, and the American female by showing her ruthlessness and almost masculine ambition.   Under the spell of a woman, the hero is capable of extraordinary exploits while treading the edge of the
precipice, doomed, like Hemingway's heroes, to fall off.

Lust, pride, money, murder (and other forms of
violence), food, religion--these are the simple raw materi-

als of Cain's novels.   Sex is deliberately implied when not
directly expressed; as the characters lunge "rapidly from motive to act," the terrific pace of the narrative and the dialogue, with their climaxes, is almost sexual.   Pursued in an
atmosphere of evil, inseparable from violence, sex has an
aura of the unnatural.   Murder and money make the sex possible.   Few writers permeate their characters' consciousnesses
so thoroughly with the smell, the hot-reaching anticipation,
the grubby feel of money.   The reader shares the urgency of
the single-minded struggle for money and sex.   The characters refer to their perfunctory and animalistic lovemaking as
"holy"; love and murder produce a sham religious mystique.
Cain has been accused of obscenity.   That he seldom describes
the sex act in detail and never uses four-letter words suggests
his skill in creating the illusion of full description.   "Criticism in this country," he has cause to remark, "is incorrig-
ibly moralistic."

        If sex is at the heart of Cain, it is not always sordid.
Throughout most of Galatea, the relationship between Duke and
Holly is mostly platonic, mainly because of the fat in which Holly
is encased; Duke, having helped her reduce, falls in love with
her.   Like most of Cain's other women, Mildred enjoys sex without guilty aftermaths, but probably her sense of owning material
things means more to her than sex.

        But generally, the sex (or love) has something ab-
normal about it.   While the murdered body of Nick is still
warm, Frank and Cora make love near his carcass.   She
begs him to rip her open.   "Hell could have opened for me
then, and it wouldn't have made any difference.   I had to have
her, if I hung for it.   I had her" (46).

        The heroes meet their women the way the male has
always dreamed, and a bizarre setting enhances sex--again
the wish comes true.   With his characteristically Byronic
audacity, Sharp in Serenade wins Juana in a lottery from a
bullfighter and seduces her in a rural Mexican church; in
The Butterfly, Jess's supposed daughter offers herself to him
and they make love in an abandoned mine shaft; the hero is
inclined to shift his emotions from his lover to her sister or
her daughter.   Frohock claims that the strangeness of the
scene often leads the reader to accept the author's "trickery."

        Lovemaking in Cain's work is animalistic.   Snarling
like a cougar, Cora begs Frank to bite her.   But she is capable of spontaneous kindness too: she tucks in Frank's
blanket as he lies on a stretcher in the courtroom moments

after he has double-crossed her.   Frank repeatedly says he
smells Cora.   Love for him is somatic: "I wanted that woman so bad I couldn't even keep anything on my stomach" (7).
Again Frohock objects--Cain appeals to our prurience, our
instinctive curiosity about sacrilegious behavior, our fascination with the ways of unknown, glamorous savages.   "Sex,
so conceived, is inseparable from violence" (9).   I think
Frohock is right, but I also see evidence that Cain intends
to dramatize the reality of these elements in our lives.   Cain
is one of those rare writers who can use effectively the method
of extremes to render a truthful quality of human nature
and experience.   But these elements function even more appropriately when viewed primarily as creating the energy that
keeps the "pure" novel moving.

        In most of Cain's novels, money is at the heart of
the love affairs.   A crime for money and freedom must be
committed, the lovers feel, before the course of love can run
smoothly.   Usually the husband, the major obstacle, is im-
potent in a sense, the highly charged wife desires a potent
stranger to take over as in The Postman and Double Indemnity.
In only a few of the novels do the lovers commit no crime,
and only in three is there no desperate love situation from
beginning to end.   None of the lovers pay legally for the
crimes they commit for love and money; most set in motion
circumstances which bring about their own horrible destruction.

        An atmosphere of evil, often pagan in mood and en-
hanced by superstition, overhangs the tales and broods over
the events.   In Serenade, a shark is a general symbol of
evil and violent death, hidden by beauty, and a big, incredibly ugly iguana symbolizes the dark animal in us all.   The
butterfly   mark on Katy's child's stomach is a sign of evil
because it is the focus of the mystery of progeny which
causes several murders.   But rare moments of beauty and
peace dispel the aura of evil for a while.   When Jack Dillon
sees the beautiful green luna moth, he feels what "I imagine
other people" feel "when they think about God in church" (4).

        Out of the murderous love affairs grows a kind of mys-
tique.   Two people strive antisocially to be together, excluding all others from their world.   Ironically, their actions
increasingly shrink that world, until both their mutual goodness
and evil come face to face; they achieve what is goodness and
purity for them in the very moment when their evil threatens
to destroy them by turning them against each other--an evil
they have forgotten while creating the goodness.

The classic illustration of this irony is found in The
Postman. For Frank and Cora, sex, religion, and murder
are facets of the same passion. They have moments of child-
like innocence; for them, erotic sensations are analogous to
religious ones; and they continually betray and forgive each
other. Grasping for heaven on earth, they sleep with the
devil: "Well, what the hell? We're together, ain't we?"
(88). Swimming in the ocean just after they are married,
she puts his love to the test when she tells him she is pregnant. He can leave her and swim to the shore or help her
to get back. He promises to help her. They are happy in
the knowledge that just as they took a life, they are giving
one back. Now they go through a purification ritual in the
ocean. Frank dives deep under the water. "And with my
ears ringing and that weight on my back and chest, it seemed
to me that all the devilment, and meanness, and shiftlessness,
and no-account stuff in my life had been pressed out and
washed off, and I was all ready to start out with her again
clean, and do like she said, have a new life" (114-15). Driving back to the restaurant, they have a wreck and she is
killed. On the eve of his execution he puts his faith in a
mystical reunion with her. The pagan element clashes with

The pagan element clashes with the Christian in Serenade,
especially in the Mexican church scene in which Sharp and Juana
make love. Food, like God, is often associated with illicit love,
as when the ritualistic preparing and eating of the iguana precedes
the lovemaking. In his relationship with the primitive Juana,
Sharp regains his masculine singing voice and is freed of homosexual desire. She is also the source of a kind of religious peace
and wholeness. "Then I'd take her in my arms, and afterward
we'd sleep, and I felt a peace I hadn't felt for years.... I'd think
about the Church, and confession, and what is must mean to people who have something lying heavy on their soul.... And mostly
I understood what a woman could mean to a man" (136). She is
the physical agent of redemption too, for when Winston threatens
to bring out the homosexual in Sharp again, Juana kills her rival
in a mock bullfight with a sword.

Sex, the desire for purity, the desire for money, and
the necessity to kill or use violence to attain all three are
depicted in Past All Dishonor. Love, food, and God are intricately related in Galatea too.

Until he died at the age of eighty-five in 1977, the
most durable of the "tough" novelists, Cain continued to

promise a novel of greater depth and significance.   Some
aspects of Cain's novels indicate that he deserves more careful study than a first glance at his work or his reputation may
reveal. He has always been serious about his craft. A writer of unfortunate faults, Cain is an interesting example of a
man whose American journalistic temperament has blurred his
creative field of vision.   While it may seem that neither a
serious intention nor an artistic conception lies at the heart
of any of his eighteen novels, his works do exhibit a strange
mingling of serious and of popular elements which he has
made his own.   Although his vision of life never becomes
sharply focused, controlled, or conceptualized, it is obviously heightened and exaggerated for a purpose, and it creates
an effect that is often poetic.   While Cain seldom rises above
certain commercial elements and never seems to quite step
over the threshold into art, his novels are valuable illustrations of the concept of the "pure" novel.

It is certainly his art, more than anything else, that
moves the serious reader to almost complete emotional commitment to the traumatic experiences Cain renders, and it
is this that convinces me that without his finest novels, The
Postman Always Rings Twice, Serenade, Mildred Pierce,
and The Butterfly, the cream of our twentieth-century fiction would be thinner. Straddling realism and expressionism,
he often gives us a true account of life on the American scene
as he has observed it, and in his best moments he provides
the finer vibrations afforded by the aesthetic experience.   As
an entertainer he may fail to say anything truly important
about life, but he takes us through experiences whose quality
is to be found in no other writer's work.

CHAPTER FIVE

A Comparison of Cain's The
Postman Always Rings Twice
and Albert Camus's The Stranger

In her book on Camus, Germaine Brée states that
Sartre related the style of The Stranger to that of American
novelists "and Hemingway in particular" (103n). In a conversation with me in 1965, Professor Brée emphatically sta-
ted that Camus told her he had been influenced by Cain.
Richard Lehan reports that "When The Stranger was first
translated into English, a few of the reviews mentioned
Camus's debt to James M. Cain. Professor Frohock in The
Novel of Violence in America 1920-1950 is the first critic to
maintain that Camus acknowledged Cain's influence.... There
are obvious parallels between The Stranger and The Postman
Always Rings Twice, a novel, by the way, which was extremely popular in Paris in the late Thirties" ("Camus's L'Etranger
and American Neo-Realism," 235). Camus, says Frohock,
paid Cain "the compliment of imitating him"; he admitted "to
copying certain American novels" (The Novel of Violence, 87,
95). The French edition of The Postman Always Rings Twice
available to Camus was Le Facteur sonne toujours deux fois
(Paris, 1937), in its twelfth edition by 1948. I have been
unable, however, to ascertain whether he read Cain in English or in French. Camus may have seen a French movie
version of Cain's novel Le Dernier Tournant, released in 1939.
He may also have seen the Italian version Ossessione, one
of Luchino Visconti's finest and most controversial films,
released in 1942. Visconti also directed The Stranger, re
leased in 1967.

Rayner Heppenstall, in The Fourfold of Tradition,
also links the two novels: "Formally, The Outsider [The
Stranger] is a beautifully handled exercise in tough fiction.
At the time of Camus's literary beginnings, tough American
fiction was greatly admired in France. I find English ad-

mirers of Camus shocked by the suggestion that he can have owed anything" to The Postman. "I cannot see why ... because formally," it was "original" (190).

In The Novelist as Philosopher, John Cruikshank says that the five or six years after the war was "the great period, in French novel-writing, of trial and experiment based on American models. In The Stranger ... Camus proved a forerunner in the use he made of devices borrowed from Hemingway and James M. Cain."(16). In Albert Camus and the Literature of Revolt, Cruikshank adds: "Camus makes no secret of the fact that much of his technical procedure in The Stranger is of American origin ... I myself ... suggest Hemingway and James M. Cain, rather than Farrell and Steinbeck as Camus's models for his first novel." Characteristics of the literature of revolt, as exemplified in Camus, apply as well to American tough fiction; Cruikshank observes: "emphasis on concrete situations rather than abstract attitudes .... Their dislike and distrust of abstractions has inclined them toward economical and unadorned prose.... Existentialism ... emphasizes the priority of existence over essence and the concrete over the abstract.... A concern then with things, with material objects rather than ideal essences" (162-63).

In The Stranger Camus seems actively and acutely aware of the force of Hemingway's stylistic credo as expressed in A Farewell to Arms: "There were many words that you could not stand to hear and finally only the names of places had dignity.... Abstract words such as glory, honor, courage, or hallow were obscene beside the concrete names of villages, the numbers of roads, the names of rivers, the numbers of regiments and the dates" (191). This passage is descriptive of Cain's and the hard-boiled writers' style; their characters do not show their feelings, or rather show feelings that most people aren't accustomed to seeing expressed.

I have failed to find in any of Camus's writings a reference to Cain; his biographer, Herbert R. Lottman, does not trace the Cain influence. But when one reads A Happy Death, the novel he wrote before The Stranger, about a man named Mersault who resembles the young Camus himself, along with the first volume of his notebooks, one can well imagine the decisive effect The Postman might have had.

Camus started A Happy Death in 1936 when he was twenty-three. In Part One ("Natural Death"), Patrice Mersault, a low-wage Algerian office worker, shoots and

kills Zagreus, a legless millionaire. The next four chapters
flash back to show Mersault's daily life (as in The Stranger,
published in 1942), then his jealousy-plagued affair with Marthe (who resembles Marie in The Stranger). Marthe introduces him to Zagreus, who was her first lover; Mersault
and Zagreus have long philosophical discussions, with inter-
ludes of mutual self-analysis. As in The Stranger, Mersault's
salvation pivots on an act of murder, premeditated in this
early novel, impulsive in the later one.

In Part Two ("Conscious Death"), Mersault, already
feverish with pleurisy, goes to Prague, wanders further north,
then back to Algiers, where, in the House Above the World,
he enjoys almost ideal friendship with three girls. He mar-
ries Lucienne, whom he meets in town; a period of solitude
follows--he communes with nature. Finally, after an impru-
dent swim in the sea, he dies of pleurisy, fully conscious
and happy.

A Happy Death fails most miserably, and, when compared with the later works, most interestingly, on the level
of style. This passage illustrates Camus's style: "the gran-
diose and grotesque baroque perspectives affected Mersault
as a kind of infantile, feverish, and overblown romanticism
by which men protect themselves against their own demons."

In the notebooks, Camus expressed his aspiration to
short-circuit the immature writer's natural impulse to write
about himself and become an objective writer. Many of A
Happy Death's faults derive from Camus's failure to achieve
that aim. Essential episodes conflict in tone and function with
gratuitous episodes. In attempting to grasp everything, Camus
lost everything.

Because A Happy Death grew out of a shallow philosophical paradox (money can be the root of all happiness) and
a romantic formula abstracted from human experience (the
happy man merges his being with nature) characters and epi-
sides seem sometimes contrived, sometimes incidental; philosophical passages diminish our sense of the living presence
of the characters. On the other hand, the optimistic concept
of the absurd in The Stranger, a near-perfect philosophical
novel, emanates with fictive logic from character and action
masterfully fused.

Cruikshank reports that Camus regretted "the widespread influence of the 'tough' school ... on his French

contemporaries. " He felt that the French novel was being
"diverted from its traditional path and severely impoverished. "
He even regretted the influence of Hemingway. Ultimately,
the methods of the hard-boiled novel, which Camus himself
used in The Stranger, do more harm than good; for such methods produce one-dimensional, cinematographic characters
who are very animated but who lack human substance and
flesh. To Cruikshank The Stranger suggests three observations on this kind of novel. (1) "Characterization is alien to
the absurdist novel. " (2) "Events do not conform to any co-
herent pattern in the eyes of the absurdist onlooker. " (3)
"The absurdist novel not only turns away from character-
analysis and plot-construction; it holds in deep suspicion the
very medium that the novelist is bound to use" (Albert Camus,
162-63).

In The Rebel, Camus sums up his judgment of the
American "tough" novel. By using the technique of objective
description, Camus's work suggests that men are to be entirely defined "by their daily automatisms. On this mechanical
level men, in fact, seem exactly alike, which explains this
peculiar universe in which all the characters appear inter-
changeable, even down to their physical peculiarities. This
technique is called realistic only owing to a misapprehension. "
Stylization in the novel is arbitrary, and is born of a volun-
tary mutilation of reality. For the tough writer, it would
seem, it is the inner life more than external forces that
disrupts human actions and relationships. "The life of the
body, reduced to its essentials, paradoxically produces an
abstract and gratuitous universe, continuously denied, in its
turn, by reality. This type of novel purged of interior life,
in which men seem to be observed behind a pane of glass,
logically ends, with its emphasis on the pathological. " This
abstract universe is populated by a great many "innocents. "
"The simpleton is the ideal subject for such an enterprise
since he can only be defined--and completely defined--by his
behavior. He is the symbol of the despairing world in which
wretched automatons live in a machine-ridden universe, which
American novelists have presented as a heart-rending but
sterile protest" (265-66).

Camus apparently felt that there was little point in
writing more than one novel using this method. Cain's feeling was similar when he observed that there were few natur-
als like The Postman. Camus's method and style became
more complex and dense; so did Cain's, off and on, though
with strikingly less success. In The Magician's Wife (1965)

one observes what happens when Cain himself takes The Postman as a model and rewrites it; he cheapens what was almost cheap to begin with; everything that might have gone
wrong in The Postman goes sickeningly wrong in The Magician's Wife. Camus would have found nothing in that novel to
suggest a direction for a novel of his own. Cain, by the
way, has said, "I never read Camus" Paris Review, 135).

Despite the testimony of Germaine Brée, Lehan, Frohock, and Cruikshank, and the speculations of critics like
Heppenstall, there will, of course, be those who will resist
the idea that Camus even read Cain's novel, much less con-
ciously (or even unconsciously) used it as a model for The
Stranger. As a matter of fact, neither in his published notebooks, in which he discusses the genesis of The Stranger.
nor in any of his other writings with which I am familiar does
Camus even mention Cain or his novel by name. Thus the
following survey of the similarities and contrasts between
The Postman and The Stranger is necessarily offered as, at
most, circumstantial evidence that Camus used Cain's novel
as a model--though if he did his accomplishment is not at
all diminished.

From the very first line it is obvious that Frank is
a misfit--in society's, the reader's, and his own eyes: "They
threw me off the hay truck about noon" (3). But Meursault's
opening lines suggest only to the reader that something is
wrong with the protagonist: "Mother died today. Or, maybe,
yesterday. I can't be sure." His status as outsider is concealed from society and from himself until he commits a
criminal act, the meaning of which he ultimately understands,
though that meaning remains concealed from society (except
to the extent that millions of readers, as members of society,
come to know the significance of the act). Frank threatens
society by his actions; Meursault by his attitudes. Like all
Cain's characters, Frank acts on a motive; Meursault does
not. Though Frank refers to his past as a hobo and a petty
criminal, and though Meursault offers a few vivid details of
his life with his mother and a striking anecdote about his
father, neither has a past, except as it functions directly in
the progression of the present. As a proletarian bum, Frank
satisfies a narrative function; but since Meursault's life must
be made philosophically relevant to the lives of most people,
Camus makes him a petty bourgeois bureaucrat. According to
Lehan, both are "passive heroes who respond to immediate
stimuli" automatically and very physically; though both kill,
both generally "react rather than act" (235). Frank loves the

open road--a traditionally American, not to say romantic,
attitude; he moves on the fringe of the social structure.
Meursault is in love with the sun, a Mediterranean, animal
obsession; he sits on his terrace or lies on the beach, a
spectator of society, who wants to be left alone. Unlike
Frank, who is generally free and mobile, Meursault is sed-
entary; thus one understands that certain aspects of Frank
Chambers thrive in seemingly ordinary men. Like Meursault, millions securely within the social structure resemble
Frank in many ways; no family, no creeds, no responsibili-
ties, no interest in politics. Both lack ambition: Frank
wants the freedom of the open road rather than a respectable
business with Cora; Meursault shows no interest in his boss's
offer to advance him by transferring him to Paris. Both
simply satisfy their animal needs: they eat, drink, smoke,
and fornicate. But Frank's frequent urge to vomit stresses
his completely visceral life, while Meursault's constant head-
aches foreshadow a shift of emphasis from his body to his mind.
Frank's defense against life's pressures is also physical: violence. Meursault's defense is mental: indifference. Ultimately,
however, this indifference is transformed into the resignation
and exhilaration of the absurd man. But Frank is himself, unconsciously, an absurd man. As Frohock says, "A Cain character, like a good existentialist, is what he does" (97). Thus,
generally, Frank and the Meursault of the first half of Camus's
novel are ontologically very similar, except that Frank is bound
by motive, Meursault by cause and effect. Lehan, too, sees
Frank and Meursault as absurd heroes, differing from characters
in Gide. The difference is that Frank and Meursault are "far
more elemental and behavioristic." While the characters in many
other contemporary novels are "aware of the absurd, only Meursault, like Jake Barnes and Frank Chambers, lives in a one-to-
one relationship with this kind of world" (235). But from the
killing on to the peroration, Meursault, unlike Frank, becomes
increasingly articulate about his relationship with man and his
place in the universe.

        Both Cain and Camus employ retrospective narration.
Frank and Meursault (at least in the first half of their stories) narrate in the same manner: without reflection, each
line moving forward, with almost no reference to what has
happened previously, not even within the present time of the
novel. To demonstrate Meursault's immersion in his own
present, Camus uses the historical present several times;
it also lends immediacy in the absence of narrative interest.
Cain, too, shifts tense, but only at the end where it is most
effective for his purposes as a novelist. Frohock (among

others) objects to being told in the final pages that Frank has
been writing his story: this revelation makes the novel too
artificial and unrealistic. But he does not make a similar
charge against Camus. Is Meursault talking to himself all
of the way through? If so, Camus is more artificial than
Cain. Is he talking to the reader? If so, it seems to me
that Camus is being absolutely artificial, although that is not
necessarily a negative factor. In a sense, one overhears
Meursault's inquiry into the silence of himself, which subtly
shifts into an inquiry into the silence of the universe. The
ambiguity serves Camus's purpose. And Cain's device is
equally justified, given his objective. The first-person point-
of-view technique in Cain creates a tension between the speak-
er and his listener. Frank's and Meursault's blunt narration
do violence to the reader's emotions; but Meursault's goes
further by doing violence to many of the reader's stock attitudes. Cain's technique of immediacy reveals the situation
through the narrator; Camus's reveals the narrator himself.
It is as though Meursault is reacting now, not, like Frank,
looking back from the death cell; sometimes it seems Meursault is reacting the following day, and even later the same
day. Frank and Meursault respond only to the essentials, as
seen most strikingly in the opening twenty-five pages of both
novels; the stylistic similarities are remarkable. Cain's
technique of understatement enhances the stark situation;
Camus's goes further and suggests a philosophical attitude
about life. Their selective handling of banalities enhances
the effectiveness of both understatement and the unsaid.
Cain's "no comment" style is sustained throughout; Camus's
shifts in midnovel as Meursault becomes more aware and
more and more articulate.

    Cain is famous for the pace he sustains in The Post-
man. Camus also manages to keep the reader moving so
rapidly that he is hardly aware of the absence of plot in the
narrative sense. Both novels progress along a similar plot
line, except that what is being set up in The Stranger is not
primarily a killing but a philosophical action, while The Postman illustrates a situation solely. In both novels a murder
is followed by a trial and a waiting for execution in the death
cell. The killings and the trials are, of course, very different. But the structures of the novels are similar: in The
Postman, the killing occurs a little beyond a third of the
way into the novel, while in The Stranger, it occurs exactly
in the middle; the two novels are almost exactly the same
length. The technique of narrative compression is skillful
in both, though Camus's skill is perhaps the more subtle.

But Cain's skill in making sudden narrative transitions is
more obvious since he has a more complex plot to develop.
Both novels are held together partially through a complexity
of motifs; both use animal motifs; Cora is a cat, and Meursault, in his animal passivity on Sunday on his terrace, is
likened to a cat.

In both novels the locale is simple: a highway roadside tavern, with brief scenes in Los Angeles; a rest home
in the country and Meursault's own room, with brief scenes
in Algiers; the courtroom and prison cell appear in both
novels. The time span in both is brief, though less time
transpires before the murder in The Stranger. The lovers
in both novels go twice to the beach, a place of comfort,
peace, sensuality, mindlessness, tranquility; the beach scenes
are very similar. In both novels, the beach is also the
scene of the crime and of a kind of redemption. Months
after his crime, Frank experiences a feeling of rejuvenation
in conjunction with a feeling for Cora's pregnancy. "I looked
at the green water. And with my ears ringing and that
weight on my back and chest, it seemed to me that all the
devilment, and meanness, and shiftlessness, and no-account
stuff in my life had been pressed out and washed off, and I
was all ready to start out with her again clean, and do like
she said, have a new life" (180). The inception of Meursault's
redemption as a human being is simultaneous with his crime.
"And so, with that crisp, whipcrack sound, it all began. I
shook off my sweat and the clinging veil of light. I knew I'd
shattered the balance of the day, the spacious calm of this
beach on which I had been happy. But I fired four shots more
into the inert body, on which they left no visible trace. And
each successive shot was another loud, fateful rap on the door
of my undoing" (76). Having moved from unconsciousness to
consciousness, Meursault comes keenly to the verge of his
redemption in the final passage: "It was as if that great rush
of anger had washed me clean, emptied me of hope, and,
gazing up at the dark sky spangled with its signs and stars,
for the first time, the first, I laid my heart open to the
benign indifference of the universe. To feel it so like myself,
indeed, so brotherly, made me realize that I'd been happy,
and that I was happy still" (154).

The execution of the crime in Cain takes a long time;
the literal crime in Camus's novel occurs very quickly, but
the revelation of Meursault's other, social, "crimes" is
prolonged. Frank kills on the second of two deliberate, premeditated attempts; on the beach, Meursault has three encounters with the Arab who threatened Raymond, Meursault's

friend; progressively fewer people are involved, until only
Meursault and one of the Arabs confront each other.   Appropriately for a novel of action, Frank kills at night, while
bright, common sunlight illuminates Meursault's commonplace act, and light is appropriate for a novel of self-
knowledge.   In The Postman, Frank commits a "perfect,"
premeditated murder; in The Stranger, Meursault performs a
gratuitous, spontaneous, impulsive, irrational killing.   Frank
kills with a wrench, a tool of his trade as a mechanic; ironically, Meursault uses a revolver, a more criminal weapon.
Nick is simply in Frank's way; the Arab causes Meursault
pain as the sun glances off his knife into Meursault's eyes;
Nick stands between Frank and sexual gratification; the Arab
stands between Meursault and animal pleasure--shade, relief
from the sun.   "Camus's man is very much less like Hemingway's Morgan than like Cain's Frank Chambers," says Frohock.   "Chambers kills the Greek clearheadedly enough, of
course; there is none of Meursault's irrationality in the actual
performance of the murder.   But still the motive is as irrational, as buried in instinct, as is the motive of Meursault.
Chambers smashes the Greek's skull ... for exactly the
same reason that a young bull elk kills the old herd bull.
What significance the act has is biological, not moral.   Cain's
violence is 'animal violence' in the exact meaning of the
words" (206).   Frank and Meursault kill with little hesitation.

　　　　To Frank, Nick is a friend, then an obstacle, then a
victim, then a kind of ghost (unconvincingly for the reader,
Frank has nightmares); to Meursault, the Arab is a stranger,
an obstacle, a victim, then, indirectly, a savior.   At the
funeral of his victim, Frank breaks down and weeps; at the
funeral of his own mother, Meursault does not.   Frank is
not as cool as Meursault; when things go wrong, he breaks
down; and he is almost as sentimental about love as is Meursault's Marie.   Meursault's failure to cry at the proper time
contributes to his conviction.   To have Cora and be free,
Frank deliberately kills.   Meursault, who takes sex, like everything else, as it floats his way, would never kill for Marie;
but, though he appears to kill for no reason at all, existentially the act serves to free him from his old self.

　　　　Both authors proceed from certain assumptions about
their readers.   Cain assumes that they will sympathize and
identify with the killer-narrator in spite of and because of
his acts yet agree with Cain that he should die in the end.
Camus assumes his readers will be repelled by Meursault's
attitudes, gradually won over to sympathy, then suspend

judgment of the act while others are so stupidly judging it. But
Camus goes further. His novel is deliberately <u>about</u> attitudes
and assumptions, worked out through Meursault's relationship
with society. In having the court judge Meursault for his
attitudes rather than his criminal acts, Camus puts society on
trial. Cain, of course, has Frank convicted only for his acts.
Frank's conduct is intended to do temporary violence to certain of the reader's moral attitudes. Camus deliberately and
directly does permanent violence to more serious and representative normal attitudes and assumptions--about mother, marriage and love, friendship, jobs and ambitions, God--but not
so much through overt acts as through Meursault's responses
to ordinary human events, as in the novel's opening line.

     Even the assumption that one should weep at the fun-
eral of one's mother is hinted at in <u>The Postman</u>. But the
funeral is that of Cora's, not Frank's mother. Just as the
characters around Meursault assume that he is grief-stricken,
so Frank assumes that Cora is: "I guess you had a bad time
of it, hey?" Her response is as cold as Meursault's: "It
wasn't very pleasant. But anyhow, it's over" (156). Both
Frank and Cora show a little more sensitivity when they
view their victim's corpse in the morgue: "Off to one side,
on a table, was something under a sheet ... She began to
cry when they lifted the sheet off, and I didn't like it much
myself" (80). The hypocrisy and fickleness of moral attitudes
is briefly suggested in the funeral scene in <u>The Postman</u>.
The preacher makes cracks about how the Greek was killed
until someone passes around a newspaper, declaring that
Frank and Cora are innocent. The difference is that Frank's
own responses to a funeral are superficial, socially negotiable,
while Meursault reacts in a way that would make him a stranger even to Frank.

     Assumptions about masculine fraternity are also ex-
amined in the two novels. Just because they work and sing
together, Nick assumes that Frank is his friend; Raymond
immediately assumes certain intimate agreements between
himself and Meursault, based on masculinity and the dark
underside of social relations, for Frank takes his wife and
kills him; like Raymond, Nick depends upon mechanical social notions. Basically, Meursault is as estranged from Raymond as he is from the Arab; ironically, it is the Arab who
becomes his friend, for the Arab is the involuntary means of
Meursault's existential enlightenment. In a different way,
Nick is the means of Frank's temporary sexual happiness.

There are two trials in <u>The Postman</u>; the second and
most crucial is compressed, in the service of narrative
thrust, into a paragraph. The single trial in <u>The Stranger</u>
is the major narrative event in the second half of the novel,
and it releases the meaning of Meursault's behavior. If one
includes the episodes between the first and second trial as a
kind of trial in itself, then the second half of <u>The Postman</u>,
too, is a trial. Cora puts Frank through an ordeal like a
trial, keeps him captive, so to speak, in the restaurant, until
she absolves him in their ocean swim. Kennedy's blackmail
is similar to the social blackmail the magistrate attempts on
Meursault, for the magistrate says, in effect, "If you will
pay society in lies, society will give you back your freedom."
Sackett's interrogation of Frank is somewhat like the magistrate's interrogation of Meursault, seemingly friendly at first;
and the prosecutor's questioning of witnesses at Meursault's
trial is just as damning as Frank's answers to Sackett. But
while Cain is interested in the intricacies of the law, and in
showing how Frank gets tangled up in them, Camus shows how
Meursault becomes entangled in the intricacies of moral attitudes which are alien to him. Cain's brief satirical cuts at
the conduct of justice may have suggested to Camus the possibilities for a whole sequence of ironies: "The magistrate
sat on a platform ... and in front of him was a long desk
that ran clear across the room, and whoever had something
to say hooked his chin over the desk and said it." Again,
"the cop told them to raise their right hand, and began to
mumble about the truth, the whole truth, and nothing but
the truth. He stopped in the middle of it to look down and
see if I had my right hand raised. I didn't. I shoved it up,
and he mumbled all over again. We all mumbled back."
And "When they got done, all that the whole bunch had proved
was that the Greek was dead, and as I knew that anyway,
I didn't pay much attention." When an insurance agent who
is testifying begins to sound as though he is giving a sales
talk, the magistrate holds up his hand. " 'I've got all the
insurance I need.' Everybody laughed at the magistrate's
gag. Even I laughed. You'd be surprised how funny it sounded"
(106-10). Unlike Meursault, Frank does not feel de trop
in the courtroom but, as a disaffiliated, "disinherited" proletarian, he is. The prosecutor and the judge call Frank a
mad dog; a similar charge is made against Meursault. Each
is to die, ironically, for a crime other than the one he really
committed--Frank for killing Cora, not for killing Nick;
Meursault for failing to weep at his mother's funeral, not for
killing the Arab. Neither is dead as the novels end. In <u>The
Postman</u>, Cain does not assume that readers will disapprove

of the judges; Frank is guilty, the victim of irony rather
than of a cruel and stupid judiciary. Camus, however, ex-
pects his readers to condemn Meursault's judges for trying
him on superficial issues. Meursault's innocence nevertheless is often misinterpreted as Camus's condonement of the
act, or at least of the character of Meursault, but characters
in Camus's other novels indicate that he did not approve of
the Meursault who killed the Arab; Meursault is only relatively better than his judges. Both Frank and Meursault take
responsibility for their crimes. Frank refuses to take the
easy way out by blaming his unconscious, as the fratricide in
the next cell does. Camus introduces a patricide, and Meursault's prosecutor attempts to link the two crimes, charging
that Meursault's authorized the other man's crime. The killing of the father is more meaningful to Camus's novel than
is the fratricide to Cain's.

Both novels conclude with a scene in a death cell.
Many things in The Postman parallel the much longer death-
cell section of The Stranger. In both novels, the cell is anticipated: confinement in the restaurant for Frank, who wants
to be out on the open road, presages the death cell; the
deathwatch room at the old people's home and Meursault's
own cell-like room at home more aptly anticipate his death
cell. Frank is about to be hanged, Meursault to be guillo-
tined. But Frank knows his execution date, while Meursault's
predicament is more like the daily predicament of all men:
He does not know exactly when "they" will come for him,
though it will be in the night, softly.

In the death cell, Cora is more important to Frank
than God's love and forgiveness; he asks those who read his
account to pray that he will be with her; he seems to reject
Father O'Connell's means of comfort as a viable substitute
for dreams of Cora. Frank admits a token belief in God as
a means of getting what he wants--Cora, in life or death.
Camus deliberately rejects such sentimental self-deception;
Meursault's very longing for Marie is preferable to a futile
hope of having her in heaven or hell. He tells the priest
that one strand of a woman's hair (Marie's) is worth all his
certainties; Frank merely poses the possibility that the priest
may cross him. While Cain relates sex to religion (when he
is happy with Cora, Frank feels as though he is in church),
Camus places sex above religion. Following his rejection of
the priest and religion, Meursault opens his heart to "the
benign indifference of the universe" (154).

Each novel projects a prophetic sense of doom and anticipates in many ways the hero's fate. The very manner
and method of telling conveys a sense of the inexorable.
Chance and coincidence help to create this aura of inevitability. It is by pure chance that the drifter Frank meets Nick
and Cora; it is by pure chance that Cora is killed and her
note is found in the cash register. Through the pattern of
premeditated events run the coincidences and chance happen-
ings that result in Frank's undoing. It is by chance that
Meursault encounters the Arab and is carrying a gun. Upon
the series of chance moves in The Stranger, the prosecutor
imposes premediation: "What he was aiming at, I gathered,
was to show that my crime was premeditated" (124). The
general critical interpretation seems to be that Meursault's
act is involuntary manslaughter and thus rather accidental,
and from this premise proceed interpretations of the rest of
the novel; others discuss it as a fated act. But Camus's
novel is much more meaningful if Meursault's act is deliberate in a profoundly existential sense, for it enables him to
live the essence of the absurd vision by the end of the novel.
Whereas Meursault begins to experience self-knowledge in his
death cell, Frank goes to his death more deluded than ever,
but it does not follow that the reader shares the delusion.

"Cain's novel," says Lehan, "of course, lacked a symbolic structure and metaphysical frame of reference" (235).
Cain's has bogus religious overtones; Camus's has a serious
philosophical intention. Camus begins with the world as it is
given in The Postman; but by the end Camus has suggested a
point of view that is never quite explicit though always implicit in Cain. But if Cain moves toward a pure novel, Camus,
with his philosophical concerns, moves toward the antinovel,
as described by Cruikshank. The pure-novel characteristics
of The Postman are carried forward only in the first half of
The Stranger, and in the second, Camus begins to develop a
philosophical point of view that affects man in every phase
of his life; thus The Stranger, ultimately, is the very opposite of the pure novel. Like Lehan, Frohock comments ad-
versely on the lack of a large philosophical dimension to The
Postman. But in noting that Frank passes "rapidly from motive to act," Frohock seems unaware that this is an important
theme and intention of existential literature. "The difference,
of course, is one of the intention," says this critic. "Camus is
building his novel around the idea of the absurdity of life"
(95). So is Cain, though less explicitly; to achieve something
one does not have consciously to intend it. Whether Cain is
aware of it or not, the persistence of this theme is real
enough in his work forcibly to show that he feels the truth

of the concept but does not feel compelled to preach it.   The absurdity of man's existence, often remarked by Cain's characters, does seem to reveal itself most horribly in the wish that comes true with breathtaking suddenness.   Having gotten what they wished, Frank and Cora, and their counterparts in other novels, create for themselves a more painful hell than existed before, more than they can survive.   Both Frank and Meursault hope for an appeal, but Camus goes further: Meursault gets some comfort from his new awareness of himself in the universe.

While one cannot say with certainty that Camus deliberately used The Postman as a model, it can be said that every element in Camus's novel that parallels an element in Cain's novel has been transformed into something finer. What in Cain is crude and mechanical (but in its own way superb) is elevated and ennobled in Camus.   If The Postman is a tough-guy novel of action, The Stranger is a serious novel of character, with implications about the human predicament.   But though a profound philosophical concept may make for good philosophy, it does now endow a novel or work of art automatically with value.   It is not Camus's philosophy alone that makes The Stranger a greater novel than The Postman.

CHAPTER SIX

The Aesthetics of Popular Culture: Cain's Serenade and
Morris' Love Among the Cannibals

The articulation of a popular culture aesthetics that
is at once based on, but that significantly departs from,
traditional concepts is the most difficult and most urgent business before scholars of popular culture as a new discipline.
After two decades of aggressive study of popular culture, one
ought to consider dropping the notion that absolutely anything
goes because, as everyone knows, popular culture, an infant
field of study with modest pretentions, is not very well defined.
Why not begin to define it? A common aesthetic base for
popular culture is lacking. To create a flexible system of
popular culture aesthetics, one must go back to the origins
of aesthetics and reassess, repossess, and assimilate.

An outside observer may regard efforts to formulate
even a tentative aesthetics for popular culture a joke. One
risks sounding pedantic, and further risks refutation in pedantic terms. These are notes on an approach to the task of
formulating a basic popular culture aesthetic from which one
can venture as far as one wishes, and about which one can
debate and argue.

Those who study popular arts, it should be noted at
the outset, are schizoid. One must always take this condition into account as one examines the products of popular art,
especially when one formulates basic principles, as here in
the realm of aesthetics. Schizoid because The Postman Always Rings Twice, for instance, was not written primarily
for those who write about it, nor is it they who respond most
fully to its primary elements. On the other hand, in the
realm of so-called "high art," those who formulate and evaluate are also those for whom the works examined are primarily produced. In the study of popular art, those who
formulate and evaluate are not those for whom the work was
primarily produced--except in childhood (and so, nostalgia is

93

an active element for the scholar, as for the primary consumer). Still the context is larger, richer for the scholar;
the experience is conscious for the scholar, unconscious for
the ordinary consumer.

Popular culture scholars have yet to get in touch with
their schizophrenia: as children they were products of popular
culture; as adults they were trained, many of them, in high
culture, while retaining their affection for and interest in
popular culture. Now, they return to popular culture as students and scholars. Consequently, in this transitional stage
in the history of popular culture studies, one often speaks out
of a kind of aesthetic schizophrenia with a forked tongue,
Since their personal and professional interest is in both the
popular culture in which they were spontaneously nurtured and
the high culture which they willfully acquired, they must,
constantly, by deliberate acts of the imagination, look at popular culture from the point of view of makers and consumers
(who include their younger selves).

One problem is to determine what concepts and emotions are to be considered in formulating an aesthetics and
in what order of importance; what degree of impact can be
assigned to each? And should one account for the special
experiences of the student or scholar of popular culture in
the formulation, and if so, to what degree? Should one attempt to show that there is good art, bad art, and nonart?
Should one set out to show that popular art is the same as
high art, just not as intense? Or should one articulate a new
aesthetics for a new sensibility? Is there a new sensibility?
Or only a new attitude, new superficial characteristics?

"Aesthetics" or "art" is so often used as an honorific
term rather than simply as a descriptive term that one
shouldn't invite scoffing criticism for a loose appropriation
of the term and its precepts. One doesn't want to seem to
be borrowing luster, any more than one wants to put oneself in a position of apologizing. One should neither praise
a work the high culture condemns nor support the condema-
tion itself. Popular culture scholars strive for a sound,
inclusive, though always flexible, system of aesthetics.

In the writings of Leslie Fiedler, Kenneth Rexroth,
Harry Levin, even Rene Welleck and T.S. Eliot, one finds
scattered comments on the validity of studying popular culture
--for social or moral insight into the times. Is popular
culture the number two brain in the withering tail of the

dinosaur?   Or the antennae of the race?

In "Aesthetics of Popular Culture," John Carvelti says,

> Many scholars and enemies of popular culture share
> the assumption that a popular work is successful
> because it embodies or expresses the values of the
> popular mind in a particularly effective or direct
> fashion. Thus, social and psychological analysis is
> the dominant mode of interpretation in dealing with
> this kind of material. So high art is commonly
> treated as aesthetic structure or individual vision;
> the popular arts are studied as social and psycholo-
> gical data (Journal of Popular Culture, Fall, 1971).

Cawelti is right to contend that this is a pseudodistinction,
for high art too is valued as social and psychological data.
One should add that popular art is too seldom studied in its
aesthetic aspects.   Cawelti says, "We ought to ask what
psychological process or mechanism makes the expression
of commonly held values popular with the public.   Is it simply
that we find comfort in repetitions of received opinions?"
That is an apt description of what happens in high art, also.

The general assumption is that extrinsic factors are
not important in traditional aesthetics.   In popular art,
however, they may prove to be inseparable from aesthetic
concepts.   An examination of the forces that produced popular
culture originally may suggest concepts for an aesthetics.   In
his monumental history of American popular culture, The
Unembarrassed Muse, Russel Nye discusses five main forces
that produced and determined the character of popular culture:
increased population; mass production; urbanization; universal
education; and the electronic revolution. It is necessary to
investigate such questions as, How does the economics of
distribution affect the popular culture experience aesthetically?

Research into those and other areas can easily be done.
The use of statistics is more suitable for popular art than
high art.   Interviews with consumers about taste and nostalgia
as determinates could be conducted. This work would involve
the methods of social science.   The environment in which the
work is obtained and the imagined environment in which the
work is made should be examined.   Experimental research
into the physical energy expended in experiencing a popular
culture product should be conducted.   That would involve
the biological sciences.   Santayana and Dewey based their

aesthetics partly on biology. The emphasis so far has been as Cawelti observed, mainly social. One must now go very deeply into the psychology of perception (Gestalt psychology will probably prove the most useful); the psychology specifically of reading, of moviegoing (see Pauline Kael's reviews), of looking at pictures, and of two areas high culture neglects: nostalgia and taste. Research into the psychic energy expended in experiencing a popular art product should be pursued. The psychological context of a specific work, though not overtly encouraged by the work, comes into play in our experience of popular culture. Study the social, moral, political values involved in the popular culture experience. All these extrinsic factors are important and we should study their effect on the aesthetics of popular art. But these secondary factors now dominate the growing interest in popular art.

Here are some of the insights of a new aesthetician, Susan Sontag:

> "Interpretation is the revenge of the intellect upon art."
> "Interpretation takes the sensory experience of the work of art for granted, and proceeds from there."
> "We need an erotics of art."
> "In art, 'content' is, at it were, the pretext, the goal, the lure which engages consciousness in essentially formal processes of transformation."
> "To speak of style is one way of speaking about the totality of a work of art."
> "Transparence is the highest, most liberating value in art. Transparence means experiencing the luminousness of the thing in itself, of things being what they are."
> "What is needed is a vocabulary--a descriptive, rather than prescriptive, vocabulary--for forms.
> "The function of criticism should be to show how a work of art is what it is, even that it is what it is, rather than to show what it means" (Against Interpretation).

The aesthetics of popular art ought to deal directly only with those components that may be considered part of the aesthetic experience. The task of other branches of popular culture study is to deal with other aspects: social, political, psychological.

One may start from traditional aesthetics as it deals with high art and discover what is unique or different in the

popular art aesthetic experience, and then adapt to popular
culture those traditional concepts that are found to apply.
What are the major, basic principles of traditional aesthetics,
as well as the new aesthetics? It's difficult to talk about
aesthetics because subjective criteria can easily contradict
objective criteria in this field so that theories are always par-
tial and tentative.   And should be.   The literature itself is
extremely small,   not only in philosophy but in each branch
of the arts.   About sixty years ago Clive Bell reassured us
that the literature is so small, aesthetics stands in no danger
of being accused of turning out more nonsense than any other
field.   That's still true.

      Before reviewing some of the traditional aestheticians,
one might look at a few recent observations.

      Although the concept of "camp" always threatens to
obscure the articulation of popular art, Susan Sontag's famous
"Notes on 'Camp'" may be turned around to provide genuine
insights into the nature of popular culture.   For instance, in
her very first note, she makes a claim that popular culture
studies should make:

            "Camp is a certain mode of aestheticism.   It is
            one way of seeing the world as an esthetic phenom-
            enon."
            "Style is everything."
            "The camp sensibility is one that is alive to a double
            sense in which some things can be taken."
            "Camp turns its back on the good-bad axis of or-
            dinary aesthetic judgment."
            "One cheats oneself, as a human being, if one has
            respect only for the style of high culture."
            "Camp taste is, above all, a mode of enjoyment,
            of appreciation--not judgment....   Camp
            taste is a kind of love ... for human nature.
            It is neither cynical nor scornful."

No set of notes on popular culture aesthetics as brilliant as
those Sontag has given us on the camp sensibility exists.

      Sontag's comments on art in general are suggestive
for popular culture, too.   In "One Culture and the New Sensibility," she attacks the insistence on a division between high
and low culture, a distinction "based partly on an evaluation
of the difference between unique and mass-produced objects."
Recent serious art is:

> "reasserting its existence as 'object' (even as man-
> ufactured or mass-produced object, drawing on the
> popular arts) rather than as individual personal ex-
> pression."
> "Because the new sensibility demands less 'content'
> in art, and is more open to the pleasures of 'form'
> and style, it is also less snobbish, less moralistic
> --in that it does not demand that pleasure in art
> necessarily be associated with edification."
> "The affection which many younger artists and in-
> tellectuals feel for popular arts is not a ... spec-
> ies of anti-intellectualism ... It does not mean
> the renunciation of all standards. The point is
> that there are new standards ... of beauty, style,
> and taste. The new sensibility is defiantly pluralis-
> tic; it is dedicated both to an excruciating serious-
> ness and to fun and wit and nostalgia."

So is the study of popular culture.

For over twenty years, Leslie Fiedler has been scat-
tering insights into the aesthetics of popular culture thoughout
his writings. Thirteen years ago, in Love and Death in the
American Novel, for instance, he said, in the course of a
discussion of popular culture elements in the fiction of Nathanael West:

> "S. J. Perelman has been conducting a strange ex-
> periment, whose end is the transformation of Sur-
> realist gallows humor into commercial entertain-
> ment .... The avant-garde images of twenty-five
> years ago ... have become now the common
> property of gift shoppes and greeting-card racks,
> fall as stereotypes from the lips of hip 12 year olds
> ... In Lenny Bruce, for example, the distance be-
> tween literature and entertainment, high art and low
> comedy threatens to disappear" (489).

A popular culture aesthetics must account for this close affin-
ity between popular culture and the avant-garde.

Leslie Fielder could write an aesthetics of popular
art if he only would. But one suspects his moral and sociological bias keeps him from sustaining interest in a system-
atic aesthetic. Meanwhile, as he machine-guns the glass
facade of American culture, he will continue to contribute
scattered insights into the problem.

The aesthetics of popular culture arises out of limitations of forms, conventions, tastes, imposed from without by
society and audiences upon popular culture artists. Russel
Nye, in the Introduction to The Unembarrassed Muse (or the
bare-assed muse) says:

> The popular artist hopes to do the very best he can
> within the rigorous limits set by his situation.
> His accomplishment must be measured by his skill
> and effectiveness in operating within the boundaries
> of the majority will and the requirements of the
> mass media, nor should he be expected to do other-
> wise . . . . This does not mean that what the popu-
> lar artist does is not worth doing, or personally
> unsatisfying, or aesthetically bad, or commercially
> cheap. . . . With skill and talent alone, sometimes,
> a popular artist may transmute mediocre material
> into something much better than it is, or even good;
> the gradual improvement over the years of stand-
> ards of performance in the popular arts pro-
> vides sufficient proof of this. . . . Contemporary
> popular artists have developed tremendous tech-
> nical skill, and their sophistication and subtleties
> of performance are much greater than their pre-
> decessors.

Popular art then gets its effect by permissible devia-
tions from limitations. High art gets its effects in tensions
between external and internal limitations.

One finds both in a study of the commedia dell'arte
and silent slapstick movies. Each characteristic of commedia
dell'arte and of silent slapstick comedy is an externally imposed or self-imposed limitation forcing the actor to develop
skills that enable him to control and turn to advantage those
limitations. Convention imposed upon the commedia the limitation of the five masks. Technological limitations imposed
upon slapstick movies the limitation of silence. The commedia
imposed upon itself the task of improvised action and dialogue.
Silent slapstick movie comedy imposed upon itself the limitation of improvised action, which added to the burden of
compensating for lack of sound. The freedom of improvisation was exercised within the limitations, externally and in-
ternally imposed by a set of stereotyped characters, costumes,
acting areas, etc. At every point in a comparison of commedia dell'arte and silent slapstick, we find forceful substantia-
tion of a basic aesthetic principle: that the source of genius

is an ability to control externally imposed limitations and recognition of the necessity to risk imposing certain limitations
upon oneself in order to realize one's potential. The actor
must subordinate himself to the demands of his fellow actors,
while giving his own abilities full scope and thrust. Since his
character was set, his only freedom is in his art. His task
is to control that freedom. One sees this principle at work
even in the amorphous, rowdy, self-indulgent audience, which
helps create, then insists on the observance of, certain con-
fining conventions; but within these conventions, the spectator's
imagination is encouraged to range and soar. Because of the
film medium's greater visual realism, the moviegoer parti-
cipates more easily but less imaginatively than the theatergoer (Madden, Harlequin's Stick, Charlie's Cane).

    Neither Russel Nye, Ray Browne, Marshall Fishwick,
nor other major popular culture scholars, excepting John
Cawelti and Alan Gowans, go deeply into the problem of aesthetics. Pathfinders, they leave mapmaking to others. The
Journal of Aesthetics and Art Criticism is a better source for
discussions of the aesthetic aspects of popular art than The
Journal of Popular Culture. One finds very few theoretical
pieces on aesthetics in the back issues of JPC. Several
essays have "aesthetics" in the title, but, like the titles of
stories in Secret Confessions, fail to deliver.

    "The Concept of Formula in the Study of Popular
Literature" (JPC, Winter, 1969) by John Cawelti proves to
be an exception to that observation.

        "Most works of art contain a mixture of convention
        and invention...."
        "A formula is a conventional system for structuring
        cultural products. It can be distinguished from
        form which is an invented system or organization."
(Cawelti's distinction between form and formula is descriptive,
not qualitative.
        "Formula represents the way in which a culture has
        embodied both mythical archetypes and its own pre-
        occupations in narrative form."
        "Formulas are important because they represent
        syntheses of several important cultural functions
        which, in modern cultures have been taken over
        by popular culture."
        "Formula stories seem to be one way in which the
        individuals in a culture act out certain unconscious
        or repressed needs."

"To analyze these formulas we must first define
them as narrative structures of a certain kind and
then investigate how the additional dimensions of
ritual, game, and dream have been synthesized into the particular pattern of plot, character, and
setting which have been associated with the formula. "

More recently, in "Notes Toward an Aesthetic of Popular Culture" (JPC, Fall, 1971), Cawelti suggests that the
auteur approach to film should be adapted as one method of
analyzing all popular art.

"The auteur critics, finding artistic value and interest in the Hollywood film, have created a new mode
of analysis based on the individual stylistic characteristics and thematic interests of the director as
they show up in his collective works. "
"The auteur is an individual creator who works within a framework of existing materials, conventional
structures, and commercial imperatives, but who
nonetheless has the imagination, the integrity, and
the skill to express his own artistic personality in
the way he sets forth the conventional material he
works with. "
"The artistic dialectic between auteur and convention, the drama of how the convention is shaped to
manifest the auteur's intention, excites our interest and admiration. "

One must take all these approaches into account, treat-
ing all as provisional ways of seeing, but striving at the same
time for concepts on which a consensus can be reached.

"Aesthetics" originally meant "perception, " and through
use became associated with the study of artistic beauty and
how it happens. Before the term or its precepts may be used
in the study of popular art, one must decide whether popular
products can be termed beautiful. Implicitly, though too seldom explicitly, even high art aestheticians suggest that it can.
Susanne Langer cautions, though, that "old words with new
meanings are treacherous. " What is needed is not meanings
for old words--rather a putting to new use of old concepts.

Even in high art, the purely aesthetic pleasure is rare.
The effort to merge high art aesthetics with popular art, blurs
lines that ought to remain clear, because an aesthetics should
account for all the differences one enjoys between high art

and popular art as well as the similarities that clarify the
nature of each. One needs not only to review the major
principles of Plato, Aristotle, St. Thomas Aquinas, Kant,
Schopenhaur, Nietzsche, Croce, Santayana, Dewey, Bosanquet, Clive Bell, Roger Frye, Collingwood, Susanne Langer,
the existentialists and the phenomenologists, but to reexper-
ience them imaginatively, within the context of popular culture studies. (For a quick review, see Masterpieces of
World Philosophy, edited by Frank N. Magill. Quotations
that follow are from commentaries in MWP). Many of the
great aestheticians do allude to the problem of the so-called
lower degrees of art, and not always disdainfully.

Here are some of the major principles of the aesthetics of Santayana, Croce, Tolstoy, Bosanquet, and Dewey.

In The Sense of Beauty (1896), Santayana says that
"nothing in principle can be ruled out as a possible object of
beauty." Consider James M. Cain's The Postman Always
Rings Twice. But not everything is equally beautiful. Consider Camus' The Stranger modeled on The Postman. Our
subjective biases (taste) discriminate degrees of beauty.

> "Our preferences are ultimately nonrational; things
> are good because they are preferred."
> "Beauty is pleasure objectified; when a spectator
> regards his pleasure as a quality of the object he
> sees, he calls the object 'beautiful.' "
> "Form pleases when in perception the excitation of
> the retinal field produces a semblance of motion
> while the mind synthesizes the elements perceived."
> "The aesthetic component 'expression' is the re-
> sult of the emotional associations excited by con-
> templation of the aesthetic object."

Tolstoy's What Is Art? appeared in the same year as
Santayana's book.

> "Art is the intentional communication of feeling."
> "The artist uses colors, sounds, words, or other
> material to create an object which will provoke in
> the spectator the feeling the artist himself once had
> and which he intends to pass on to others."

(Art communicates an actual experience.)

> "True art is not only sincere but infectious. The

more widespread the appeal and effectiveness of the
the work as a means for communication of feeling,
the better the work is as art. "

(Art and life are not separate, the aesthetic experience
is not unique.)

"The highest art is that which communicates the
feeling of brotherhood and the love for one's neigh-
bor. "

Often, it the more esoteric aesthetician who provides
us with clues to the aesthetics of popular culture.   Thus,
Tolstoy is less suggestive than Croce, who said one must
"treat works of art not in relation to social history but as if
each a world in itself, into which from time to time the whole
of history is concentrated, transfigured and imaginatively
transcended in the individuality of the poetic work, which is a
creation, not a reflection, a monument, not a document. "

Croce's great work is _Aesthetic_ (1901).   "Art is an
intuition and intuition is the expression of impressions. "

"A sense impression or image becomes an expression, or intuition, when it is clearly known as an
image, and when it is unified by the feeling it represents. "

(Croce replaces the concept of beauty with expression.)

"What gives coherence and unity to the intuition, " says
Croce, "is feeling, " not ideas.   Out of pure intuition the
artist produces an image that is expressive of feelings.
"For Croce intuitive knowledge is the possession of images,
but of images clarified by the attention of the spirit, freed
of all vagueness in the act of apprehension. "   Pure lyrical
intuition is a work of art, consisting of a "complex of images
and a feeling that animates them. "   "All true intuition is
art. "   This concept does not exclude popular art.   Only intuitions are works of art; physical objects are not.   Thus,
for popular art, we do not concentrate only upon the produced
object but the intuitions that occur in the maker and the
consumer's spirit.

"Works of art exist only in the intuitions that
create or recreate them. "
"Intuitions are of individuals, not universals. "

"The externalization of works of art by the fashion-
ing of physical objects which will serve as stimuli
in the reproductions of the intuitions represented is
not art. "
"Art is not concerned with the useful, the moral,
or the intellectual. "
"The fanciful combining of images is not art. "
"Art is neither history, nor philosophy, nor natural
science, nor the mere play of the imagination, nor
feeling in its immediacy, nor instruction, nor rhetoric, nor morality. "

Croce cautions us not to mistake the intellectual for the artistic, the concept for the intuition.

"The theoretical activity of the spirit has two forms:
the aesthetic and the logical: the practical activity
is composed of the economic and the moral. "
"Knowledge has two forms ...   it is productive of
either images or concepts. "
"The aesthetic values are the beautiful (the expressive) and the ugly: the logical values are the true
and the false: the economic values are the useless and the useful: and the moral values are the
just and the unjust. "

The science of art, says Croce, "is the perpetual systemati-
zation, always renewed and always growing, of the problems
arising from time to time out of reflection upon art. "

Bernard Bosanquet is an English philosopher about
whom one seldom hears--the way one hears about Croce and
Dewey--but one would do well to rediscover and to study his
Three Lectures on Aesthetics (1915) closely.

"Aesthetic experience is distinguishable from other
experience in that it is pleasant, stable, relevant,
and common. "
"The aesthetic experience is contemplative, not
practical; it is organizational, and both personal
and general. "
"The aesthetic response is a response to form and
substance in an appearance, requiring the imagination, and resulting in the pleasant awareness of a
feeling embodied in the appearance. "

Bosanquet stresses the importance of the imagination,

which is the mind considering possibilities (similar to
Croce's "intuition"?). "The most satisfying aesthetic experience is realized when the artist forms his work in harmony
with the character of his medium." Bosanquet was intrigued
by the demands of the individual medium. "The properties
of the medium lead the artist to do certain things that another
medium would not lead him to do." Obviously, this notion
applies even more to popular culture's many media than to
high culture's. "In its proper sense, beauty is what is common to artistic products insofar as they are excellent; beauty
may be easy or difficult; difficult beauty is characterized by
intricacy, tension, and width--that is, it is complex,
provokes heightened feeling, and demands breadth of interest."
Bosanquet argued that easy beauty that is pleasing to every-
one--to a wide community--is not to be denigrated; "it can
be beauty of the highest type." A single work of art may be
difficult to the person with a wide range of interest and easy
to the ordinary person. "The aesthetic experience is a response to what is there, to what the object is in itself, and
not to some relation the object has to other things or other
people." Here Bosanquet anticipates Sontag.

    John Dewey, reviewing Bosanquet's History of Aesthe-
tics, observed: "The entire conception ... of a fixed distinction between the realm of art and that of commonplace
reality seems to me to need a good deal of explanation." To
understand the aesthetic, Dewey said, on another occasion,
"one must begin with it in the raw." Dewey's Art as Experience (1934) synthesizes the best insights of Santayana, Tolstoy, Croce, Bosanquet, and gives them new emphases within the context of Dewey's own revolutionary ideas. The work
as a whole is a primer of popular culture aesthetics that
not only preserves the most relevant of high art aesthetics but
reactivates it in a realm of richer possibilities. "Aesthetic
theory should explain how works of art come into existence
and how they are enjoyed in experience. How is that something produced to fulfill a need becomes in addition a source
of aesthetic enjoyment? How is it that ordinary activities can
yield a particular kind of satisfaction that is aesthetic." To
Dewey, "the most vital arts are popular music, comic strips,
newspaper accounts of crime and love, articles on the intimate
doings of popular entertainers," and everyday, ordinary activities themselves. Vital art is connected with the actual
processes of living.

        "Any experience that combines memory of the past
    with anticipation of the future, and is an achieve-

ment of the organism in the environment in which it
functions, is an aesthetic experience."
"Art is to be understood as an experience made
possible by the organizing and unifying process in
which the artist engages.   The spectator meets the
interest of the artist with an interest of his own in
the reciprocal process of going through a similar
operation."
"Art supplies mediums of communications, making
community of experience possible."

Art is an experience of everyday life--the aesthetics of the
moment.

To review this review:

Santayana: "Beauty = pleasure objectified."
Tolstoy: "Art = human communication."
Croce: "Intuition = expression" (a charged image
in the mind).
Bosanquet: "The aesthetic experience = a feeling
of pleasure that is rechargeable, self-sufficient,
and common."
Dewey: "Art = an individual experience" (which is
the interaction between organism and environment).

Each of these principles can be employed in formulating a popular art aesthetics.   How are these principles to be
adapted to the different nature of popular art?   The popular
aesthetics experience, a study of traditional aesthetic theories
will reveal, is neither worse than nor the same as the high
art aesthetic experience--it is simply different, but not entirely.

One can learn a great deal also from outright enemies
of popular culture studies and from high art aestheticians who
embark upon slumming expeditions, such as Abraham Kaplan.
His essay, "The Aesthetics of the Popular Arts" (Journal of
Aesthetics, 1964), is essential reading for all students of popular culture, especially of its aesthetics.   By popular art, he
doesn't mean pop art, or camp, or bad art, or merely minor
art, but "midbrow" art.

"Aesthetics is so largely occupied with the good in
art that it has little to say about what is merely
better or worse, and especially about what is worse

... the priest must become learned in sin. Artistic tastes and understanding might better be served
by a museum of horribilia, presented as such.
It is from this standpoint that I invite attention to
the aesthetics of popular arts. "

The context for everything that follows is Kaplan's negative
attitude implied in that beginning.

If one ponders imaginatively his assertions, one may
see whether they cannot be adapted, not just turned upside
down, but adapted to make more positive statements about
the popular art experience: "My thesis is this: that popular
art is not the degradation of taste but its immaturity. " (Popular culture can study taste more effectively and with more
relevance than high culture can.)

"Popular art is never a discovery, only a reaffir-
mation. "
"What popular art schematizes it also abstracts
from a fully aesthetic context .... Popular art uses
formulas, not for analysis but for the experience
itself. "

(Cawelti has given us a workable approach to formula as part
of a popular art aesthetic.)

"Popular art is doubly derivative: art first becomes
academic and then it becomes popular. "
"What is unaesthetic about popular art is its formlessness. It does not invite or ever permit the
sustained effort necessary to the creation of an artistic form. But it provides us with an illusion of
achievement while in fact we remain passive. "
"Aesthetic perception is replaced by mere recognition. "
"On the psychodynamic level, the aesthetic response
is replaced by a mere reaction. "

(Perhaps it would be helpful to formulate an aesthetics of
reaction.)

"In the taste for popular art there is a marked intolerance of ambiguity. "

(Popular art creates ambiguity among works in a particular
area rather than within a single work.)

"Popular art is simple basically in the sense of
easy."
"Popular art, far from countering boredom, perpet-
uates and intensifies it."
"The skill of the artist is not in providing an experience but in providing occasions for reliving one."

(Is that what is meant by entertainment?   An aesthetics of
entertainment--as it also, sometimes, involves elements of
instruction--may be useful.)

"Popular art easily becomes dated, as society
changes its conventional associations."

(Some of it, but not all; just as Bulwer-Lytton et al., became
dated, but not Dickens.)

"Popular art wallows in emotion while art trancends
it, giving us understanding and thereby mastery of
our feelings as it finds them, formless and immature," and sentimental.
"Popular art seeks to escape ugliness, not to transform it."
"Popular art depicts the world, not as it is, nor
even as it might be, but as we could have it."

(This gets one into the importance of accounting, in one's
formulations, for the popular artist's assumptions about his
audience.)

"The self-centeredness of popular art is the measure of our own diminishing."

"There is a time and place even for popular art,"
Kaplan concludes.   He, too, we suspect, enjoys the pleasant
dreams of popular culture, but can be grateful only when he
has awakened.

"Aesthetics of the Popular Arts" is an ironic title,
for Kaplan shows, to his own satisfaction, that the popular
culture reaction is everything the aesthetic response is not.
Kaplan's half-hearted defense, then, turns out to be a full-
scale attack, with a reluctant admission that the popular arts
deserve study, probably for nonaesthetic reasons.   But close
examination of his assertions reveals more positive insights
into the way a genuine popular aesthetic experience occurs.
Kaplan's brilliant attack is the single most effective essay to
account for in the popular culture aesthetics.   No one has

come up with a positive statement of aesthetics as persuasive and well-articulated as his attack.

It is probably in John Dewey's pragmatic analysis of the aesthetic experience that one will find the most powerful refutation of or means of adapting the criticisms of Kaplan and other critics of popular culture. Reading Kaplan and Dewey side by side, one may see the positive face of Kaplan's negative judgments. From the beginning, simultaneous acceptance and rejection of popular culture has been the double vision of popular culture studies. But effective attack or defense or mere explanation must start with some positive concepts about the subject, not Kaplan's negative prescriptions.

Among recent books the one that comes nearest to dealing with Kaplan is Alan Gowan's very well-argued The Unchanging Art: New Forms for the Traditional Functions of Art in Society (1971).

> "To know what art is, you must define what it does. You can define art only in terms of function. High art historically grew out of low art, and the functions of low art have remained unchanged throughout history."

Although Gowan emphasizes the social and practical functions of art, his book is very suggestive about the nature of popular culture aesthetics.

2.

The aesthetic attitude of high culture is effort, of popular culture is receptivity. "The aesthetic attitude is the first requirement for the experience of aesthetic pleasure, and sometimes seemed," says Langer, "even to be the active source of it." This emphasis on attitude describes perfectly the way most people approach a work of popular art. If, for instance, when we approach The Postman, we lack an aesthetic attitude, we will not experience the novel's aesthetic qualities consciously.

Popular culture aesthetics can help to illuminate high art aesthetics. Bosanquet argues that "the aesthetic experience can best be understood by considering simple rather than complex examples." Popular art provides occasions for studying some of the traditional concepts of aesthetics in

purer form.   In the past few decades, high art has been over-
whelmed by nonaesthetic demands on it--psychological, then
sociological, now political; a set of extrinsic concerns different from those in popular art has commanded attention.   Perhaps in contemplating a popular culture work which can have
no overtly serious "expressive" or secondary associations,
one experiences the pure whatness of it and can come closer
to aesthetic pleasure than one does in serious works--which
one approaches with expectations of receiving a rich cluster
of secondary values: themes, ideas, symbols, etc.   Perhaps
popular art comes closer than high art to art's sake.

In introductory courses, should one teach great novels
for their own sakes?   Or should one expose students to all
the forms and types that they will encounter throughout their
lives?   Why not develop in them an ability to analyze and
understand their enjoyment and the sources of their interest
in--or their dislike and rejection of--popular fiction?   Let
each student find his place on a spectrum of quality and proceed from there.   The teacher can become a mediator between serious and popular fiction.   If students understand the
nature of all fiction, they may learn to distinguish, and perhaps discriminate with feeling and intelligence among the
great variety of fiction of the past and the present offered
within today's media-centered culture.

What is most important for undergraduates trying to
understand the nature of fiction is that one emphasize not the
individual novel--a teacher's choices are often arbitrary--
but that one emphasize the medium itself, so that having
looked at the way novels achieve their effects, the student is
better able to respond to whatever novel he may be told or
choose to read, whether it's The Stranger or The Postman
Always Rings Twice, Pride and Prejudice or Love Story.
If in fiction studies the emphasis is upon teaching an understanding and appreciation of the nature and the techniques of
fiction, and not upon specific high culture novels, then a study
of those techniques in their simpler uses in popular novels,
alongside serious novels, is one way to achieve that purpose.

Popular writers should be studied on their own
merits.   But comparative studies of popular and serious novels
may enhance understanding of each type: The Foxes of Harrow
by Frank Yerby and World Enough and Time by Robert Penn
Warren; Peyton Place by Grace Metalious and Winesburg,
Ohio by Sherwood Anderson; The Razor's Edge by W. Somerset Maugham and Siddhartha by Hermann Hesse; To Kill A

Mockingbird by Harper Lee and The Heart is a Lonely Hunter by Carson McCullers; Rebecca by Daphne Du Maurier and Jane Eyre by Charlotte Brontë. It is clearly interesting and instructive to compare popular novels with each other, Cain's with McCoy's, Chandler's, Hammett's, and Jay Dratler's (his Dudes in Thunder shows Cain's influence). Niven Busch's Duel in the Sun, 1944, is a Western version of The Postman; Busch coauthored the movie script for Cain's novel. Cain said of Duel in the Sun, "I wish my name were signed to it instead of Busch's." It is also interesting and instructive in many different ways to compare popular novels with "serious" novels, Cain's The Postman not only with Camus' The Stranger, but also Camilo Jose Cela's The Family of Pascual Duarte (1942). Such comparisons reveal that serious and popular novels employ almost all the same artistic elements, techniques, devices, and contain many of the same social messages, though with contrasting degrees of complexity and for very different ends. Of course, some elements are experienced only in one, and not in the other. But comparisons help to illuminate what makes each a good example of serious or popular fiction.

A discussion of a popular novel can make students see in crude but sharp relief the more basic techniques that are common to both formula and serious stories. To test the validity of this claim, I went back to my own book on Wright Morris and my book on Cain, written a decade apart, compared my chapter on Morris' "technique" with my chapter on Cain's "craft" and discovered that sure enough I had used almost exactly the same aesthetic concepts in discussing the works of Cain as I had Morris. Only a few concepts applied to Morris and not Cain. And each, as individual but different artists, had forced me to create new terms for what each had uniquely done. But Morris remains a master serious writer, Cain a master popular novelist, with no blurring of the lines between.

> I raised my eyes to see--the way a man meets his fate in the movies--a woman, a young woman, who had just entered the room. The directness of her gaze caught me unprepared. I returned it, that is. The word chick--the word I rely on--did not come to mind. This tremendous girl--the scale of this girl made me step back a pace to see her-- wore a flower in her hair. That's all I could tell you. I turned away at that point to collect myself.

It took me more than a moment. The jigger-size
glass that held my tequila was slippery on the outside from what I had spilled. You know the feeling you have that in your grasp, within your grasp,
you have the dream that has always escaped you--
followed by the feeling that your eyes, and your
heart, have cheated you again. When I turned she
was gone. Gone. Had she really been there? I
walked back to the main hall where I could see up
the curve of the stairs....   Looking up the flight
of stairs it occurred to me that I wouldn't know this
girl by how she looked--I didn't know how she look-
ed--I would only recognize her by how I felt. How
did I feel? The way I often feel in elevators
(38-39).

Compare and contrast that passage with a similar passage by
a different writer.

I was in Tupinamba, having bizcocho and coffee,
when this girl came in. Everything about her said
Indian, from the maroon rebozo to the black dress
with purple flowers on it, to the swaying way she
walked, that no woman ever got without carrying pots,
bundles, and baskets on her head from the time she
could crawl. But she wasn't any of the colors In-
dians come in. She was almost white, with just the
least dip of cafe con leche. Her shape was Indian,
but not ugly.   Most Indian women have a rope of muscle over their hips that gives them a high-waisted,
misshapen look, thin, bunchy legs, and too much
breast-works. She had plenty in that line, but her
hips were round, and her legs had a soft line to
them. She was slim, but there was something vo-
luptuous about her, like in three or four years she
would get fat. All that, though, I only half saw.
What I noticed was her face. It was flat, like an
Indian's but the nose broke high, so it kind of went
with the way she held her head, and the eyes weren't
dumb, with that shiny, shoe-button look. They were
pretty big, and black, but they leveled out straight,
and had a kind of sleepy, impudent look to them (1).

Which passage was written by a serious writer and which
by a popular writer? The first narrator feels a compulsion
to capture the essence of the experience, while the second
narrator tries rather objectively to describe the woman her-

self.   Each writer does well what he sets out to do.   The
first passage describes Earl Horter's first encounter with a
woman he calls The Greek in Hollywood in Wright Morris'
Love Among the Cannibals (1957), the second passage describes Jack Sharp's first encounter with the Mexican woman,
Juana, in Mexico City in James M. Cain's Serenade (1937).
Nearly every critic in America considers Wright Morris an
excellent serious writer.   James M. Cain is considered one
of America's most proficient popular novelists.   Neither
novel could be fully experienced without an understanding of and
a receptivity to the aesthetics of both serious and popular fiction.

Even though Morris is one of the most aesthetically
conscious novelists writing today, Cain in The Postman Always
Rings Twice has come closer than Morris to the pure novel
Flaubert wanted to write.   Benét refers to this purity
when he says that in Serenade and Postman, Cain has written
novels as "compact and deadly as an automatic."   In Cain's
best fiction, aesthetic distance is achieved and sustained partly because of his obsessively objective, neutral, dispassionate
attitude toward the basic elements of his novels.   His techniques forcibly, deliberately, and continually turn us back to
the pure experience itself.

Given the similar theme of Cannibals and Serenade and
similar characters and plot, how do the two novels differ?
In trying to determine what makes one novel "better," or simply different than another, one deals with two seldom discussed, somewhat antagonistic, but decisive problems: the effects
of technique, on the one hand, and of the reader's own taste
on the other.   One also confronts the related question: what
assumptions do Morris and Cain make about their readers?

In Love Among the Cannibals, Earl Horter, a writer of cliché lyrics, and his teammate Macgregor, a composer
of sentimental popular songs, are under contract to write a
movie musical; they spend most of their time on Hollywood
beaches, soaking up back and foreground.   One day on the
beach, Mac meets Billie, a blond Memphis "cannibelle," and
that night at a party Earl meets his own cannibal lover, a
sensuous woman whom he calls "the Greek."   Wanting to bolt
from his cliché-ridden life, Earl persuades the Greek, Mac,
and Billie to take an auto trip to Acapulco, where they spend
a couple of weeks in an unfinished villa, supposedly writing a
musical with a Mexican setting called "Love Among the Cannibals."   They have a fine time making love and lying on the

beach. Finally, Billie cajoles Mac into marrying her, and
the Greek bolts with an elderly biologist. In the end, Earl
envisions a reunion with her.

In Serenade, Jack Sharp, an opera singer, is stranded in Mexico City when his singing voice fails--a psychological
expression of his fear of responding to the homosexual advanc-
es of his conductor. As the novel begins, Jack's wish is to
regain his voice and become a great opera singer. Then he
meets Juana, a Mexican Indian whore, and his wish is to possess her magnificent body. The two wishes come true, but
when they move on to New York and the conductor's homosexuality poses a threat to both wishes, Juana kills the conductor
with a bullfighter's sword. Jack and Juana escape to South
America, but she is killed by Mexican police, and Jack gives
up singing as penance.

Most people know that Cain is also the author of The
Postman Always Rings Twice, Mildred Pierce, and Double
Indemnity. Fewer know the works of Morris, that he won
the National Book Award with The Field of Vision (1957), the
American Book Award for Plains Song (1980), and also wrote
The Works of Love, The Huge Season, The Deep Sleep, and
In Orbit, and the sales figures show that even fewer have
read his novels. Many Renaissance specialists who pride
themselves on their ignorance of the avant-garde have never-
theless read Cain. Most English teachers who hope someday
to find time to read Morris, have found time to read Cain.
After I gave a speech on Cain in 1963 to English teachers in
Ohio, the audience spontaneously rushed forward to declare
that Cain was a nostalgic part of their early literacy.

A comparison reveals that there are many popular culture elements in Morris' novels and many High Culture elements in Cain's novels. A popular song lyricist is the narrator of Morris' Cannibals, an opera singer is the narrator
of Cain's Serenade, and the two novels offer many details
about the two different types of music. Morris' and Cain's
complete works could easily provide the texts for an entire
course in popular culture. In the Cannibals, Earl Horter is,
by profession, if not by temperament, immersed in the clichés
of the submediocre mass-media culture of contemporary
America. "When the beach is crowded I listen for the up-and-
coming clichés" (24). Morris lived in Los Angeles for almost
a decade, off and on. Los Angeles, he says, "has never
ceased to attract, repel, and fascinate me as the laboratory
of the future" ("Origin of a Species," 133). All the inessen-

tial artifacts of the transitory moment are there: suntan oil,
portable radios, swimming caps with simulated hair.

Perhaps Cain's novels offer a better way of getting a
detailed picture of society than Morris', although Morris'
novels give one a deeper understanding of the spirit of the
times. In some ways the proletarian sagas of True Confessions magazines might give us even better details than Cain's
novels about the way people lived when Cain's first novel appeared in the thirties. For that reason, why don't libraries
keep back issues of True Confessions? Another social use
of Cain's Serenade, banned in some cities, was that it offered
in the thirties a portrayal of bisexuality that became a
textbook in medical schools. Popular tough-guy novels of the
thirties in general offered revelations of social disorder as
powerful as those of the serious proletarian novelists, most
of whose work is now dead, while Cain's is still in print.
Edmund Wilson said, "Cain himself is particularly ingenious
at tracing from their first beginnings the tangles that gradually
tighten around the necks of the people involved in those bizarre and brutal crimes that figure in the American papers;
and is capable even of tackling--in Serenade, at any rate--
the larger tangles of social interest from which these deadly
little knots derive" ("Boys, " 21). But, in both Morris' and
Cain's novels, social significance emerges subtly--it is not
their major concern.

Morris has had little effect at home or abroad on
writers, while the influence of Cain and the tough-guy writers
reaches beyond the American experience to Europe. Can a
history of American literature that omits Cain and other key
popular writers really claim to be a history at all? Robert
E. Spiller's fifteen-hundred page Literary History of the
United States, third edition, 1963, does devote fifteen words to
Cain.

Wright Morris' achievement is that he has been able
to project in his novels a many-faceted, seriocomic view of
the American landscape, character, and dream. Cain's
novels offer the tough-guy vision of the same elements.
Morris has focused on Nebraska, which represents conflict-
ing extremes in American land and character. Cain has focused on Los Angeles and Glendale. In Cannibals and Serenade, they cover the same ground. In Cannibals, the Hollywood beach enhances the theme of the phony present encrusted
with cliché inessentials; the Mexican beach enhances the theme
of the real present, stripped to essentials. The passage

from Hollywood to Mexico emphasizes Earl's shift from immersion in a phony present to his emergence into a real present in a primitive atmosphere that encourages the change.
Earl changes with the scene because of the Greek, who
doesn't need to change. Serenade follows a similar thematic
pattern, but in reverse. There are three distinct adventures,
beginning in Mexico, moving on to Hollywood, and further on
to New York--a more complete picture than Morris' of the
American land as it reveals the American character and the
dream. Cain shows how one man seizes the American dream
of success and how it conflicts with his dream of the primitive
woman. Serenade ends just when Jack is in a position to understand his problem; in Cannibals we follow with Earl the
process of understanding.

       In the motel in Hollywood, the Greek, a sexual dynamo,
teaches Earl the wisdom of the body; in the church in Mexico,
the body of Juana the whore puts the toro back into Jack's
voice. In Mexico, the Greek partially transforms Billie, the
Memphis belle, by making her aware of her body as a body,
as more than bait, by forcing her to defend it against the
Greek's animal violence. Just before she bolts from Earl,
the Greek almost bolts Billie. Ripping her gown, she ties
Billie from corner to corner on the bed, and "rubs the con-
tents of the nightpot ... like an ointment" into her flesh
(242). Earl is "struck by the beauty of her eyes now that
she had looked at something through them" (248). With
"blood under her nails," the "suntanned flesh of the Greek"
on her lips, Billie is a true cannibelle at least. In New York
Juana's act of violence--she kills her rival with a sword--
does not teach Jack anything, but it frees him.

       Cannibals and Serenade deal with many of the same
aspects of the American character that the authors develop
from one book to another--for instance, the figure of the audacious amateur and his ability to improvise. Morris puts his
amateur hero in a meaningful relationship--with a witness:
the hero is a character whose audacious behavior affects
others; the witness is transformed in his relationship with
the hero and begins to improvise upon a new life. Morris
emphasizes the importance of seizing the immediate present
in highly concentrated moments of love, audacity, or imagination, in the hero-witness relationship. Redefined from
moment to moment, time is the ambience in which the novels
take form. What is achieved is a community of vision. In
Cain's novels, the amateur hero's relationship is simply with
a woman, and they go on what Cain called a love-rack together

because one of them wishes for something and the wish comes
true. When the American dream comes true, it turns into a
nightmare in an everlasting present in which the lovers are
isolated from the human community. In Morris' novels, the
dream seldom comes true--the nightmare comes in the frus-
tration of a wrong dream. Cain's heroes are inside-dopesters
with an impulse to self-dramatization who speak in an aggressive voice and who fall from a height they have willfully
reached. Jack Sharp boasts superior know-how in every area
touched upon in the novel. He even tells Juana how a whore-
house should be set up, and thinks he might do it himself.
In Cannibals, the love affair of Earl and the Greek has a
comic dimension; typically, in Serenade, it is sex and violence all the way. In both novels, the theme is that a man
out of touch with himself and his masculinity can learn the
wisdom of the body from a woman who is sexually super-
charged.

        "Stripped down to the point where God had made us,
such as we were," says Earl, "we walked up the slope.   I
held her hand--I mean I reached out and took it the way Adam
would have held on to Eve" (210).   Jack tells us that Juana
was "stark naked .... There she was at last, stripped to
what God put there. She had been sliding back to the jungle
ever since she took off that first shoe, coming out of Tazco,
and now she was right in it" (45).   Both women are frank,
sexual forces, the ideal of pure sexual reality, archetypal
females.

        At middle age, Earl grasps "just one more chance"
with the Greek. She teaches him the impersonal wisdom of
the body. "This life I have is a gift," she tells him, "why
should I hoard it?" (79) as Horter does.   Until he meets the
Greek, he is too indifferent to try to bolt from the fix he is
in: mere existence in a world where nobody knows how to
live.   The Greek and the Mexican scene cause Earl to live
positively.   On the beach, "a strip of sun and sand where the
sex is alert, the mind is numb" (13).   Horter is in his territory ahead, which he recognizes by the fact he has not been
to this Mexico before, where he experiences a ceremony of
natural love, without cliché.   Sex is a new frontier, where
everything else begins, and the Greek and Juana are audacious
females who persuade the male that, on the sexual frontier,
where one may start from scratch, "the real McCoy" is
still possible.   But crossing such frontiers, one risks becoming sick: "To bolt with a woman you've got to burn certain
bridges that won't be there in case you come back" (132).

Jack's mistake is in trying to take Juana back to the world
he ran away from. When Horter asks her what she likes
about him, the Greek frankly says that he arouses her desire.
Her impersonal approach to sex keeps the affair as uncomplicated as possible. But Horter's thinking complicates his
feelings: he thinks, for instance, too much about the other
loves she has had, now has, or may have. But, when she
leaves him, he does not care who has her now. He takes
pride in his own luck. The end of Horter's sojourn in the
Mexican garden of Eden comes one night when the Greek,
nude, steps over the threshold of the unfinished villa with
nothing more to kick off, except Earl, who is no longer essential to her. For when Mac says, "It's been real, man!"
Earl is profoundly aware of just how real it has been. For
with the Greek, he has reached the point where he can cease
to speak the clichés of romance which his intellect has always
scorned. After her, Horter the essentialist will never again
be satisfied with less than the real thing. Once he has experienced the Greek, who teaches him to live in the present
without misgiving and without "bad Faith," Earl possesses a
real past: "Stripped down ... to what we referred to as
the essentials, I possessed nothing under the moon but my
past. That much I could take with me, if I cared to, and I
did" (249).

Having moved in a world of superfluity, Horter sees
the need to strip down materially and spiritually to the essentials. The conflict between the real thing and the cliché is
one between essentials and inessentials. In Mexico, Horter
is stripped, like the phony studio car, to the essentials; at
the same time, he is in the process of becoming, like the
unfinished house. "A reassembling of the usable parts, of
the functional experience, must begin again," says Morris
(Amherst Lectures, 1958). The only character already
stripped down when the novel begins, the Greek, the hero,
causes a stripping process among her witnesses and teaches
them "about loving and talking from scratch" (227).

When sex with Juana makes him break out in song and
regain his voice, Jack says, "Something in me had died. And
now that it had come back, just as sudden as it went, I was
like a man that had gone blind, and then woke up one morning
to find out that he could see" (52). Having lived in a world
of superfluity in Los Angeles, Morris showed in Cannibals the
need to strip down materially to the essentials. Stripping
down to essentials is not a conscious theme in Serenade, but
Cain, like Hemingway, demonstrates in his technique itself

how life, stripped down, feels. A major theme in all Cain's
novels illuminates Cannibals: "True beauty has terror in it"
(72), the old sea captain tells Jack; he is speaking of Beethoven's music, of the blue sea (full of sharks), of Juana (full
of Mexico), and of Mexico (full of dark forces like Juana and
sharks). Although Cain operates mainly within the realm of
terror, he strives in almost every novel to convey at the
height of terror a sense of the beautiful.

        Both writers have a rich imagination, but Morris' is
revealed mainly in his conceptions, Cain's in his choice of subject matter and in the invention of characters and situation.
A conception may be defined as a total, gestaltlike grasp of
the story that enables the author to control the development
of the situation, the characters, theme, plot, style, and technique, so that in the end they cohere, as in a single charged
image. A concept orders, interprets, and gives form to the
raw material of the story and infuses it with vision and meaning. The conception that governs Cannibals is difficult to
describe since it is expressed in every part of the novel.
It is much simpler to describe how Serenade derives from a
notion. The opposite of a conception is a notion, the kind of
clever premise that comes often and easily to the inventive
mind. A notion can usually be formulated in the question:
"What would happen if ... ?" A notion is only a launching
pad. Most stories begin with a notion; many never transcend
notion into the realm of conception. What would happen if
an opera singer who lost his voice out of fear of a homosexual inclination met an Indian whore in Mexico and a real
homosexual became the third part of the triangle? Cain's
imagination does not process in terms of conception and thus
transform his raw material, as Morris' does; rather, with
basic fictional techniques, Cain expertly manipulates and
controls all the elements for calculated effects. One speaks
of Cain's inventive powers, his structuring mind--a mind
aware of itself and of the reader's mind--rather than the
shaping imagination we know in Morris' work.

        The effect of a vision on Morris' novel is clear when
one discovers the apparent absence of a vision in Cain's.
Morris sets out with a vision and discovers through technique
new aspects of that vision in each novel. Morris' vision is
subjective, Cain's has the impersonal objectivity of the camera
eye. Cain doesn't set out with a vision--his concentration on
craft obscures the vision that does emerge for the receptive
reader. Morris' vision is a tough one, excluding sentimentality. If Cannibals and Serenade have the same themes,

what makes one different from, if not better than the other?
In the study of literature there should be less theme-monger
ing. How does ascertaining the theme of Cannibals enable one
to read perceptively either The Good Soldier or Love Story?

     One sees Morris' subtle use of techniques more clear-
ly after one analyzes Cain's craft. One way of doing that is
to analyze one's own relationship as reader with the author.
Most of the difficulty in reading Morris springs from the unusual demands he makes upon his readers: He insists that
their own creative imagination and intelligence enter into the
creative process so that they become finally cocreators--with-
out their active emotional, imaginative, and intellectual participation, much of Cannibals remains unexpressed. One understands this even better after studying Cain's Serenade.
More than with most writers, a study of the craft of fiction
itself; and in them, more than in most writers, a study of
craft requires an awareness of the fascinating ways in which
the author deliberately, and indirectly, creates a special relationship between himself and his ideal reader.

     In Serenade, Cain makes so many apt assumptions
about his readers that one is palpably aware of the author's
intimacy with the reader-community he has visualized for his
work. Cain is a performer aware of his audience. One
wants to see him do it again. As he manipulates and
reverses stock expectations and responses, his knowledge of
what his reader wants is phenomenal. Part of his ability
lies in the way he mingles serious and popular fictive elements. Even the serious reader becomes so involved that he
is unaware, until after finishing a Cain novel, of ways in
which the author's achievement may be examined technically
as literature. Sophisticated literary elements operate in
Cain, but so "naturally" that they neither tax the popular
reader's patience, nor, at first, impress the sophisticated
reader. Time magazine has said of Cain's audience: "It
is popularly supposed that people go right on reading the
thrillers of James M. Cain ... through five alarm fires."
Cain once asked me, his patience a little strained, "What is
a 'popular' novelist? The aim of art is to cast a spell on
the beholder; it has no other aim--or in other words, the
whole object of a novel is to get itself read." Ironically,
Morris the artist would like to have the same readers Cain
does, while Cain can claim many of Morris'.

     Many readers cultivate a sullen resentment of symbol-
ism. But they may feel less duped by Morris after they have
seen Cain's cruder use of symbolism. For instance, this

passage in <u>Cannibals</u> may go right past a reader: After making love, the Greek says to Earl, "You <u>must</u> eat it. You
need it.' She put her own spoon into my bowl, fed it to me.
I took a mouthful, but could hardly swallow. 'This is not the
time for your hurt feelings. <u>Eat</u>' " (98). One sees the symbolic beneficial sexual-cannibalism of that passage better
after one reads this cruder passage in <u>Serenade</u>: "All of a
sudden she broke from me, shoved the dress down from her
shoulder, slipped the brassiere and shoved a nipple in my
mouth." "Eat. Eat much. Make big toro!" Cain even provides the student with a built-in explanation. "I know now,
my whole life comes from there." "Yes, eat." (135)

In <u>Serenade</u>, Juana's car is "the newest, reddest Ford
in the world. It shone like a boil on a sailor's neck" (18).
Red is of course appropriate for Juana the whore, but it is
Jack who rams the car through the doors of the rural Mexican church, then later rapes Juana herself inside the church.
Again, the symbolism is clear enough, but the equally clear
symbolic use of a car in <u>Cannibals</u> is handled more deftly.
Cain's use of the car is for a momentary symbolic effect,
only generally related to the book's total design, while Morris'
use is intricately and organically related to the entire novel.
The movie studio loans Earl a fireman's red dream chariot,
a sports car, a monster of bad taste. It is a character in
itself. As the Greek gradually strips Earl's cliché and in-
essential attitudes away, Mexicans are stripping his studio car
in the ditch where he wrecked it; they reassemble it in the
image of their own rural culture. The car is Morris' symbol of what is wrong with Earl. But as Cain wrote to me,
"Who can't think of symbols?" Cain used certain signs and
symbols for character flaws, to evoke an aura of evil and the
unknown. The fin of the shark Earl sees as he is escaping
from Mexico to Hollywood with Juana is a manifestation of
his fear of homosexuality. When Juana shouts that he is a
homosexual, he tries to shut her off: "But one thing kept
slicing up at me, no matter what I did. It was the fin of that
shark" (134). And the big, incredibly ugly iguana that Jack
catches and eats in the Mexican church is symbolic of the
dark primitive in Juana and in himself. At the end of the
novel, Juana is being buried near the church: "As they low-
ered her down, an iguana jumped out of the grave and went
running over the rocks" (183).

Morris suggests the concept of parallels rather than
symbols. "My story beings," says Earl, "like everything
else, on the beach--a strip of sun and sand where the sex is

alert, the mind is numb. If you like parallels, the beach is
where we came in, and where we'll go out" (13). One is
freed from the tyranny of symbolism if one determines the
most highly charged images in the two novels--images that
enable one to interpret every other element: In Cannibals,
one sees the four characters lying on the beach in Hollywood
and the car in the ditch in Mexico, Earl throwing the keys
to the cannibals who were stripping it.   In Serenade, one sees
the composite image of Juana in Mexico feeding her breasts to
Jack, and Juana in New York impaling the homosexual conductor, with Sharp witnessing.

        Morris is one of the finest stylists writing in Amer-
ica. He has said that he wants to "use a minimum of words
for a maximum effect" (Twentieth Century Authors, 691). He
creates rhetorical tensions that sustain interest in the absence
of overt action. One way he makes his style active is in his
use of what I call "impingement." When the action of events
threatens to overwhelm the events of consciousness, Morris'
style reasserts the preeminence of process over raw material.
Something more impressive or vivid than the dramatic moment
impinges upon it. For instance, Morris presents the discovery of a flat tire in such a way as to make the manner of
discovering more effective that the flat itself. "A dog sniffed
around like it was time. He did it on the gas pump and then
he did it on the front wheel. It wasn't till then that I noticed
the tire was flat" (My Uncle Dudley, 63).

        Cain's style serves the very different function of de-
picting the action itself. There is a remarkable compati-
bility between Cain's raw material in Serenade and his terse
diction. It is a style, Benét said, "like the metal of an
automatic." The sense of authority we feel in Cain as he
relates action is a triumph of style. Cain is a master of
rhetoric in his use of description, dialogue, selectivity, and
compression. Looking back, we see that Cain has achieved
his effects by skillful omission, and suggestion, and condensation, "Execution" seems the best word for what he does;
he executes his moves, cleanly, sharply, "racing ahead like
a motorcycle."

        Both writers make conscious use of clichés. Speak-
ing of himself to the Greek in the third person, Horter says,
"Earl Horter, the master of the cliché, did not say to you
what he thought he was feeling, since he hardly knew, without the clichés, what it was he felt" (227). Jack tells us he
felt something similar about Juana: "I sat looking at her,

wondering why I couldn't go the whole hog, tell her I loved
her and be done with it. Then I remembered how many times
I had sung those words, in three of four different languages,
how phony they sounded, and how much trouble I had in putting them across" (63).

Morris says, in The Territory Ahead, "Every writer
who is sufficiently self-aware to know what he is doing, and
how he does it sooner or later is confronted with the dictates
of style. If he has a style it is the style that dictates what
he says. What he says, of course, is how he says it ... "
(137). No American writer's style, I think, is as perfectly
controlled as Morris'. Everything style has been trained over
the centuries to do, Morris makes it do in his novels. "In
the beginning was the word," says Morris, "and the word was
made flesh. American character emerges from the American
language, as the language emerges from the shaping imagination" ("Made in U.S.A.," 487). Morris' style--the American
language in action--conveys the informal tone and feel of a
man talking to men. He makes imaginative use of American
slang, clichés, idioms, and especially of midwestern speech
patterns and rhythms as a way of getting at the American
character. He tunes us in on the resignation, the melancholy
overtones, the subtle poetry, the humor, the shrewdness of
insight of midwestern speech. One of the major dictates of
Morris' style is his use of clichés. "The clichés told the
story" (Field of Vision, 70). "Character is revealed cliché"
("Made," 487). The cliché is symbolic of the American
dream defunct, and it is in this "dead" language of clichés
that Morris tells us of the sterility of modern life. But the
special contexts he prepares for clichés simultaneously anni-
hilate their phoniness and resurrect their original vitality;
he suggests that the dead past can be made to live again.
With clichés, Americans conceal whatever deep feeling they
have. "Clichés, bless them, both destroy life and make it
possible" ("Made," 490). Manipulating the clichés of our mass
culture and language as a witty and humorous function of style,
he turns clichés insight out. If "time past ... is a mythic
land of genial clichés" ("Origin," 128), and if "culture is a
series of acceptable clichés" (Field, 70-71), Morris' stereotyped characters cannot experience the present until they have
come to terms with the clichés that flood their everyday lives,
and stripped themselves down the the essentials. If one is
audacious enough to confront the real thing, one runs the risk
of being abandoned by the safe cliché. The real McCoy is
what one has after the cliché has been sheared off. Morris'
novels depict the process of improvisation in which the cliché

is transformed. After Morris' use of it, the cliché is never
quite the same--it is intellectually demolished and emotion-
ally transformed in the moment of usage.   The tone of the
fresh context Morris creates makes the familiar cliché sound
strange--it has a aura of having just been coined.   It never
loses the sense of wonder that gave it birth, the sense of the
unique on which it first thrived.   "Every cliché once had its
moment of truth," says Morris.   "At the moment of conception it was a new and wonderful thing" ("Made," 488).   In
carefully prepared contexts, Morris revives that "moment of
truth" in his use of each cliché.

From the common man's viewpoint, Morris describes
people who live in the mode of sentimental clichés.   With art-
ful control and contrivance, he creates a unique diction that
does with clichés three things simultaneously: 1) presents
them, as such, with a fidelity that reveals their essential
emptiness; 2) presents his characters in the language of the
clichés by which they live and communicate; but in so doing,
he 3) reveals what is genuine and viable.   In the same
moment that the cliché works against itself, it is transformed
and becomes, at times, both eloquent and significant.

In Love Among the Cannibals, Earl Horter is immersed, by profession if not by temperament, in the submediocre
mass-media culture of contemporary America; he transforms
clichés into song lyrics for mass consumption.   "If you live
in a world of clichés, as I do, some of them of the type you
coined yourself, you may not realize how powerful they can
be" (92).   He has become so saturated with clichés that
when he meets the Greek in Hollywood, dispensary of
clichés, he drives "west on Sunset to the sea, as it has
been done in ten thousand phony movies, a million phony
songs, and twice that many mortgaged cars" (72).   "What
next?" (a question Morris characters often ask) is the
title of the song Earl is improvising when he meets the living answer, the Greek.   Academic in the beginning, the question, at the end of the novel, is real.   The conflict between
the cliché and the real thing is one between the inessentials
and essentials.   By example, the Greek teaches Horter that
the "first problem, surgically speaking, is to remove the encrusted cliché from the subject" ("Made," 487).   With the
Greek, Horter improvises on the act of "bolting" from the
phony.   Free of clichés at the end, Horter can explore new
possibilities.   He has learned that "you've got to take what's
phony, if that's all you've got, and make it real" (112).

In a less deliberate and controlled way, what Morris

does applies to Jack in <u>Serenade</u> as well. Cain's situations, themes, characters, and style are cliché-ridden. "My clichés," says Cain, "are more or less deliberate. I hate narrative that is one hundred per cent distinguished. To me, it evokes utter unreality" (Letter). Like Morris, though without his special success, Cain consciously sets out to resurrect, control, and transform the cliché for expressive use. Juana is a whore with a heart of gold, but it is also the heart of a killer.

A comparison of Cain's use of literary devices reveals Morris' subtler use. What style does for Morris, devices do for Cain. The stock in trade of so-called hack writers, devices are often employed as substitutes for the imagination when it fails. But Cain's use of devices, though it sometimes suggests the hack writer, elevates the device to the status of a major literary tool. Even when one catches him employing a device, one experiences less a disruption of illusion than a deepening fascination.

One winces at failures of technique in Cain more than in Morris because there is not much more to Cain than skillful execution of technique. It is relevant to look at Cain's plots mechanically--in terms of openings, scene buildings, and endings. Reviewing <u>Serenade,</u> Dawn Powell said, "Mr. Cain's secret lies not so much in what he tells or in his prose as in a brilliant manipulation of story and a dexterous staggering of terror effect ... His words are simple but inflated with terror; the story grows in memory; its minor implications will roam through your dreams for days to come." What amazes readers most about Cain is his achievement in pacing <u>Serenade.</u> Morris, one realizes, achieves a different kind of pace.   Morris strives to articulate a vision of life from novel to novel: Cain strives simply to get the immediate story well-told. "My problem as a writer," says Morris, "is to dramatize my conception of experience, and it may often exclude, as it often does, the entire apparatus of dramatic action" (Letter). In <u>Serenade</u>, the kinetic quality of action is depleted in the relationship between Cain's raw material and his treatment of it. Technique consumes, as it is being produced, the emotional energy of dramatic event. The reader, as in <u>Cannibals</u>, does not help cause the combustion--he feels only the heat, as <u>Serenade</u> "races along like a motorcycle." But Cain makes the reader feel terror, and every device of the novel that will heighten that experience is made to work. "The worst offense of narrative, in my belief, is tepidity, and in my work, God willing, you will never

find it, whether I write of the past, present, or future. " Cain's
famous pace derives from his "morbid fear" of boring the
reader; he developed the technique of needling a story "at
the least hint of a letdown" (Three of a Kind, xv).

Morris' swift pace is generated more by the style itself than by the action it describes. It is style describing
moments of perception not action that creates the amazing
sense of motion in Cannibals. The active sensibility is action.
But Cain almost never slows down the showing to tell. What
we follow in Serenade is the spine of surface narrative action.
In the opening of Serenade, so much happens so fast, the
reader either immediately rejects what happens or willingly
suspends his disbelief and finer instincts and submits to Cain's
will. And no bossier, more willful author ever wrote--unless
he's Morris.

Serenade is neither serious nor popular; it is pure
entertainment, an experience in which strong distinctions
between one sort of reader and another seem superflous.
But as Edmund Wilson has said, "There is enough of the
real poet in Cain--both in writing and in imagination--to make
one hope for something better. " Most readers approach
Morris with aesthetic attitudes and expectations that are fulfill-
ed more fully than in most other serious writers. When
they approach Cain, they lack an aesthetic attitude, and do
not therefore experience the novel's aesthetic qualities consciously. But my study of Morris' aesthetics made me receptive to Cain's and as I analyzed Cain's aesthetics, I came
to understand and feel Morris' more fully. Both these writers
could have learned from each other, but neither tried to read
the other. Their readers may learn, among other things,
that a carefully articulated and soundly based popular aesthetics may well force a revision of the aesthetics of serious
fiction.

SELECTED BIBLIOGRAPHY

Primary Sources

For a more detailed listing of reprintings of stories, plays, essays, and of editions, including foreign, see E. R. Hagemann and Phillip C. Durham, "James M. Cain, 1922- 1948: A Selected Checklist, "Bulletin of Bibliography, XXIII (September-December, 1960), 57-61. Items below are arranged in chronological order.

BOOKS

Our Government. New York: Alfred A. Knopf, Inc. 1930.

The Postman Always Rings Twice. New York: Alfred A. Knopf, Inc., 1934.

Serenade. New York: Alfred A. Knopf, Inc., 1937.

Mildred Pierce. New York: Alfred A. Knopf, Inc., 1941.

Love's Lovely Counterfeit. New York: Alfred A. Knopf, Inc., 1942.

Three of a Kind. New York: Alfred A. Knopf, Inc., 1943. Contains Career in C Major, The Embezzler, and Double Indemnity, with Cain's preface.

Past All Dishonor. New York: Alfred A. Knopf, Inc., 1946.

Sinful Woman. New York: Avon Editions, Inc., 1947.

The Butterfly. New York: Alfred A. Knopf, Inc., 1947, with Cain's preface.

The Moth. New York: Alfred A. Knopf, Inc., 1948.

Jealous Woman. New York: Avon Book Co., 1950.

The Root of His Evil. New York: Avon Book Co., 1951.

Galatea. New York: Alfred A. Knopf, Inc. , 1953.

Mignon. New York: The Dial Press, 1962.

The Magician's Wife. New York: The Dial Press, 1965.

Cain X 3. New York: Alfred A. Knopf, Inc. , 1969. Contains The Postman Always Rings Twice, Mildred Pierce,
   Double Indemnity. Introduction by Tom Wolfe.

Rainbow's End. New York: Mason Charter, 1975.

The Institute. New York: Mason Charter, 1976.

Hard Cain. Boston: Gregg Press, 1980. Introduction by
   Harlan Ellison. Includes Sinful Woman, Jealous Woman,
   and The Root of His Evil.

The Baby in the Icebox. New York: Holt, Rinehart, and
   Winston, 1981. The short stories included are "Pas-
   torale, " "The Taking of Montfaucon, " "The Baby in the
   Icebox, " "The Birthday Party, " "Dead Man, " "Brush
   Fire, " "Coal Black, " "The Girl in the Storm, " "Joy
   Ride to Glory. " The novella, "Money and the Woman"
   ("The Embezzler") is also included. Several long com-
   mentaries by Roy Hooper.

SHORT STORIES

"Pastorale, " The American Mercury, XIII (March, 1928),
   291-95. First-person narrator, "we" point of view.
   Set in the South. Story pattern of The Postman.
   Cain's best short story.

"The Taking of Montfaucon, " The American Mercury, XVII
   (June, 1929), 136-43. Humorous first-person, autobio-
   graphical tale, based on an incident in World War I,
   told in illiterate Southern vernacular. Included in Our
   Government; reprinted twice in The Infantry Journal.
   Although the Civil War is the background for his two
   historical novels, there is no contemporary war in
   Cain's fiction.

"The Baby in the Icebox, " The American Mercury, XXVIII
   (January, 1933), 7-17. First-person, imaginative, im-
   probable, entertaining tale, with many similarities to
   The Postman, which appeared a year later. Set in Cal-

ifornia.   A study in American exhibitionist masculinity.
Reprinted five times in the forties.

"Come-back," Redbook, XXXVIII (June, 1934).

"Dead Man," The American Mercury, XXXVII (March, 1936),
    326-31.   One of Cain's best works in the third person,
    and one of his best stories (reprinted six times, includ-
    ing O. Henry collection).   Set in California.   Similar-
    ities to The Moth and "The Girl in the Storm."

"Hip, Hip, the Hippo," Redbook, XL (March, 1936).

"The Birthday Party," Ladies' Home Journal, LII (May,
    1936), 30-31, 59-60.   Cain's best third-person story.
    One of two about childhood, it involves a boy and a girl.
    Theme of masculine self-dramatization.

"Brush Fire," Liberty, XIII (December 5, 1936). 16-20.
    Third person; set in California.   Ironic tale of a man
    who saves a bum from a brush fire in the morning and
    kills him in the afternoon because the bum seduces his
    wife.

"Coal Black," Liberty, XIV (April 3, 1937), 20-22, 24.   One
    of Cain's least effective stories in third person; set in
    eastern Kentucky.   Nineteen-year-old miner and a six-
    teen-year-old girl are briefly trapped in a haunted mine,
    one of Cain's favorite sex situations.

"Everything But the Truth," Liberty, XV (July 17, 1937),
    14-17.   Less successful third-person voice than in "The
    Birthday Party."   Set in Annapolis.   A variant of "The
    Birthday Party" situation; a little boy's masculine boast-
    ing gets him into trouble, and, in this story, a girl
    named Phyllis rescues him from the scorn of his peers;
    they deceive their juvenile society into thinking that he
    is more of a hero than he is.

"The Girl in the Storm," Liberty, XVII (January 6, 1940),
    6-9.   One of Cain's best third-person stories.   Set in
    California.   Similar to "Dead Man."   A nineteen-year
    old hitchhiker and a girl take refuge from a flood in a
    deserted supermarket.   Reprinted twice.

"Pay-off Girl," Esquire, XXXVIII (August, 1952), 30, 108-9.
    First person.   Set in Maryland, near Washington, D.C.

The narrator, a twenty-five-year-old code clerk, meets
a payoff girl for bookies and frees her from her boss.
One of Cain's worst stories.

"Cigarette Girl," Manhunt, I (May, 1953), 85-89.

"Two O'Clock Blonde," Manhunt, I (August, 1953), 84-91.

"Death on the Beach," Jack London's Adventure Magazine,
    I (October, 1958), 93-101.

"The Visitor," Esquire, LVI (September, 1961), 93-95.
    Third-person tale of a suburbanite who wakes in the
    night to find a runaway tiger staring into his eyes; the
    hero subdues the tiger with a plastic bag.   Humorous,
    a sense of the absurd; embarassingly contrived ending.

"Joy Ride to Glory," published in The Baby in the Icebox
    for the first time.   Probably written in late thirties.
    An escaped convict gets caught in a storm drain.   Heavy
    irony.

PLAYS   (With the exception of three, only those plays
not included in Our Government are listed here.)

"Trial by Jury," The American Mercury, XIII (January, 1928),
    30-34.   Chapter VII in Our Government; and in Law-
    rence E. Spivak and Charles Angoff, eds. , The Amer-
    ican Mercury Reader (Philadelphia: The Blakison Co. ,
    1944).

"Theological Interlude," The American Mercury, XIV (July,
    1928), 325-31.   Theme of the dramatic appeal and sex-
    ual excitement of Fundamentalist religion; play enhances
    belief, and belief sanctifies play.   Reprinted in The
    Baby in the Icebox.

"The Will of the People," The American Mercury, XVI (April,
    1929), 394-98.   In Our Government, Chapter IV;
    and in Robert N. Linscott, ed. , Best American Humor-
    ous Short Stories (New York: The Modern Library, 1945),
    as "The Legislature."

"Citizenship," The American Mercury, XVIII (December, 1929),
    403-8.

"The Governor," Chapter III in Our Government; and in A
    Subtreasury of American Humor, E. B. White and
    Katharine S. White, eds. (New York: Coward-McCann,
    1941), 224-34.

"Don't Monkey with Uncle Sam," Vanity Fair, XL (April,
    1933), 39.

ESSAYS AND ARTICLES (Arranged to suggest concen-
    trations of Cain's interests as a journalist.)

I.   The American Character

"American Portraits. I. The Labor Leader," The Amer-
    ican Mercury, I (February, 1924), 196-200. Rather
    cynical, mocking in tone, written in the coarse language
    of the subject, starting off with witty impressions.
    Cain's description of the change in the man who slugs
    his way into the presidency of the union (changes in
    clothes, house, popular-culture tastes) evokes a picture
    of the upper-lower-class working man and his environ-
    ment.

"American Portraits. I. The Editorial Writer," The Amer-
    ican Mercury, I (April, 1924), 433-38. A witty, biting
    description of the evolution of a reporter's cynicism
    into idealism when he becomes an editorial writer.
    Compares the reporter's with the editorial writer's
    treatment of the same news event. Analysis of clichés.

"The World Hits the Trail," The Nation, CXX
    (March 4, 1925), 233. As editorial writer for the
    World, Cain ridicules his colleagues on The World for
    attacking immorality in Desire Under the Elms.

"Are Editorials Worth Reading?" The Saturday Evening Post,
    CC (December 24, 1927), 21, 38. A balanced discussion
    of the positive and negative aspects of editorial writing
    in the United States, with anecdotes out of his own ex-
    perience. The New Yorker reprinted his editorial on
    Battling Siki, a boxer, which, "it is said, almost got
    the Pulitzer Prize for the year 1925."

"Pedagogue: Old Style," The American Mercury, II (May,
    1924), 109-12. Exhibits the merciless invective of
    Sinclair Lewis lacerating a go-getter. Written when

Cain himself was teaching, the essay describes the pedagogue's "incurable hankering for the posture of wisdom." Mimicking a typical faculty meeting, he lets the
clichés roll. One of his finest essays.

"Politician: Female," The American Mercury, II (November,
1924), 275-78. Some of the wit sounds merely "cute"
today, but it is here that Cain overtly expresses a number of his attitudes about women.

"High Dignitaries of State," The American Mercury, III (December, 1924), 438-42. "It is clear that politics under
democracy, on its visible levels, is an impossible trade
for heroes. The man who seeks romance there is
doomed to disappointment.

"The Pastor," The American Mercury, V (May, 1925), 30-34.
To Cain the American pastor is ridiculous and contempt-
ible; and his role is dramatically impossible. He lacks
a sense of poetry, beauty, and imagination in his conception of religion and places of worship. One of Cain's
wittiest and most vicious essays.

"The Pathology of Service," The American Mercury, VI
(November, 1925), 257-64. "I propose herein to isolate
the bacillus of Service," says Cain, "the itch to make
the world better." Its specific cause is the idea of
Progress, its roots are in the appetite of dull people
for drama. This brilliant, scornful, antialtruistic
essay contributes to our understanding of the reformist
element in American society. It summarizes a dominant
strain in all the essays that focus on the American
character.

"The Man Merriwell," The Saturday Evening Post, CXCIX
(June 11, 1927), 12-13, 126, 129, 132. It is not sur-
prising that Cain should find William Patton, the creator
of Frank Merriwell, hero of 204 novels for boys, fascinating. They are both magnificent showoffs. Patton
dealt with the basic sources of the interest which the
American male has in masculine drama. The essay is
both a straightforward history of pulp fiction and a tribute to a one-man drama industry (about one book a week
for ten years). As for the problem of "bad" fiction,
Cain betrays no awareness that it exists.

"Tribute to a Hero," The American Mercury, XXX (November,
1933), 280-88. Nostalgic memoir of Cain's childhood in

Chestertown, focusing on a football hero who had a "yellow streak." One of Cain's finest essays.

II.   The American Scene

"Treason--To Coal Operators," The Nation, CXV (October 4, 1922), 333-34.   First of three on the drama of coal in West Virginia.   Extremely competent, tight, straight-forward journalistic prose; reports on the farcical trial in Charles Town of Walter Allen, a miner accused of declaring war on the state of West Virginia; Cain condemns management's tyranny and attacks the conduct of the judiciary.   (Forms the basis for "The Governor" in Our Government.)

"The Battleground of Coal," The Atlantic Monthly, CXXX (October, 1922), 433-40.   Well-written account of the condition of the coal industry, of the miners, repeating the story of Allen against a broader and longer presentation of the history of the industry; he also analyzes the problem and offers a few solutions.

"West Virginia: A Mine-field Melodrama," The Nation, CXVI (June 27, 1923), 742-45.   Here Cain's interest in the pure drama of events comes out; using opera motifs, he examines the common man's appetite for drama.   Both labor and management look silly.   The theme and the technique objectify his material.

"The Solid South," The Bookman, LXVIII (November, 1928), 264-69.   "It is my purpose in this article," says Cain, "to discuss certain twists in the Southern mind ... perhaps to hazard a few forecasts as to what the future may hold."   He attempts to "clear up any misconceptions that may have arisen in your mind" about notions of lawlessness, intolerance, race relations, and the backwardness of the "bozarts" in the South.   He feels that the best people should have certain rights which the worst cannot handle.

"Paradise," The American Mercury, XXVIII (March, 1933), 266-80.   In his longest essay, Cain attempts "an appraisal of the civilization of Southern California" as a part of the present American scene and vanguard of the future American civilization.   Missing in this region is a sense of the unexpected; and a terrifying sameness withers the imagination.   He demonstrates his concept of dullness as a producer of a frantic desire for drama.   With his typical American tough fairness, he enumerates the good points and the factors favoring a bright future for the region. He concludes that the future is a show worth seeing. Interesting autobiographical detail.

"The Widow's Mite, or Queen of the Rancho," Vanity Fair, XL (August, 1933), 22-23, 54. A witty, cynical look at the history of Malibu; an explanation, and an interpretation of the significance of its present image.

III. On Writing and Writers

"The End of the 'World, ' " New Freeman (March 11, 1931), 611-12. Cain's analysis of the character of the 'World' and of its editors, Herbert Bayard Swope and Walter Lippmann.

"Camera Obscura," The American Mercury XXX (October, 1933), 138-46. An important, very well-written essay about writing for the movies; an objective analysis of the medium. Cain comments on his own career and attitudes.

"Introduction," For Men Only (Cleveland: The World Publishing Co., 1944), 5-8. A likely title. Cain's choices for the collection and his comments in the Introduction on each author suggest something about his reading habits and interests. He includes stories by Irwin Cobb, Poe, Bierce, London, Alexander Woollcott, Farrell, O'Hara, John Collier, Dorothy Parker, Ben Ames Williams, Jack Boyle (Boston Blackie), Maugham, Irwin Shaw, Steinbeck, Hemingway, Fitzgerald, and Conan Doyle, along with one of his own, "The Girl in the Storm." Interesting comments on writing as well.

"The Opening Gun." The Screen Writer, I (May, 1946), 6-9. First of five articles about Cain's attempt to organize an American Authors' Authority.

"An American Author's Authority," The Screen Writer, II (July, 1946), 1-14.

"Just What Is A. A. A. ?" The Screen Writer, II (October, 1946), 1-4.

"Do Writers Need an 'AAA'?" The Saturday Review of Literature, XXIX (November 16, 1946), 9, 40-41.

"Respectfully Submitted," The Screen Writer, II (March 1947, Supplement, 12-21.

"Vincent Sargent Lawrence," The Screen Writer, II (January, 1947), 11-15. Cain pays tribute to his mentor on the occasion of his death, using a tough tone, as though he were writing about Lawrence as he felt Lawrence would like.

"Preface," Three of Hearts (London: Robert Hale, 1949), v-x. Cain expresses his special interest in the Southwest, in Sacramento, in ghost towns such as Virginia City and Port Tobacco, Maryland, and clears up popular misconceptions about ghost towns. For his English readers, he also describes the Middle West and the culture and dialect of West Virginia. Comments on his own approach to writing. See also the prefaces to Three of a Kind and The Butterfly for comments on California and on writing.

IV.　Miscellaneous

"How to Carve that Bird," Esquire II (December, 1934), 38, 140. First of three witty "how-to" essays in the tough-guy manner, revealing Cain's interest in food, an important element in his fiction.

"Them Ducks," Esquire III (January, 1935), 38, 166, 168. One of Cain's best essays.

"Oh, les Crepes-Suzettes," Esquire III (February, 1935), 33, 174.

"Close Harmony," The American Mercury, XXXVI (October 1935), 135-42. Offers important insights into another major element in Cain's life and work--music. The theme of self-dramatization is explored here, as it is in most of the other essays and articles.

"Walter Lippmann Had Style," Washington Post, Potomac Magazine (February 1, 1975), 8-11.

Secondary Sources

Annotations are made only of the more important essays

and books. An asterisk indicates essays and books devoted mainly to Cain.

Adams, J. Donald. The Shape of Books to Come. New York: Viking Press, 1944.

*Agee, James. Agee on Film. New York: McDowell, Obolensky, 1958. On Double Indemnity, Mildred Pierce, and Postman.

Angoff, Alan, ed. American Writing Today. New York: New York University Press, 1957.

Auden, W. H. "The Guilty Vicarage." In The Dyer's Hand. New York: Random House, 1962.

Aydelotte, William. "The Detective Story as a Historical Source," Yale Review, XXXIX (1949-50), 76-95. Essential. Often reprinted.

Baumann, Michael L. B. Traven, An Introduction. Albuquerque, New Mexico: University of New Mexico Press, 1976. On The Death Ship.

Bellow, Saul. Dangling Man. New York: Vanguard, 1944.

Bode, Carl. Mencken. Carbondale, Ill.: Southern Illinois University Press, 1969. Cain's comments on Mencken derived from Bode's interviews.

_____. The New Mencken Letters. New York: Dial Press, 1977. Several of Mencken's letters to Cain.

Breé, Germaine. Camus, rev. ed. New York: Harcourt, Brace, & World, 1964. On Camus and Postman.

*Brunette, Peter and Gerald and Peary. "Tough Guy: James M. Cain Interviewed," Film Comment XII (May-June, 1976), 50-57. Excellent source of detail about Cain's Hollywood years.

Buckler, William S., ed. Novels in the Making. Boston: Houghton-Mifflin, 1961.

*"Cain, James M." The New York Times. October 29, 1977, p. 26, section I. Obituary.

*_____. Publishers Weekly, CCXII (November 7, 1977),

24. Obituary.

*"Cain, James M. " Anna Roth, ed. Current Biography, 1947.
New York: H. W. Wilson Co. , 1948.

*"Cain Scrutiny. " Newsweek, LIX (April 23, 1962), 99.   Bio-
graphical details.

* "Cain's Books Popular in All Editions, " Publishers Weekly,
CLIII (January, 1948), 143. An account of the phenom-
enal publishing history and sustained popularity of
Cain's novels.

Camus, Albert. A Happy Death. New York: Alfred A.
Knopf, 1972.

_____. The Rebel. New York: Vintage, 1960 (1942, 1951).

_____. The Stranger. New York: Vintage, 1958 (1956).

*Carmody, John. "James M. Cain at Twilight Time." The
Washington Post, Potomac (January 19, 1969), 12-27.
Useful, long article with several photographs.

Cawelti, John. "The Concept of Formula in the Study of
Popular Literature. " Journal of Popular Culture, III
(Winter, 1969), 381-403.

_____. "Notes Toward an Aesthetic of Popular Culture."
Journal of Popular Culture, V (Fall, 1971), 255-68.

Chandler, Raymond. The Blue Dahlia, ed. , Matthew J.
Bruccoli. Carbondale, Ill.: Southern Illinois Press,
1976. The screenplay, with stills, and a memoir by
the producer, John Houseman, afterword by Bruccoli.

_____. "Oscar Night in Hollywood. " Atlantic Monthly,
CLXXXI (March, 1948) 24-7.

_____. "The Simple Art of Murder. " Atlantic Monthly,
CLXXIV (December, 1944), 53-9.

_____ and Billy Wilder. "Double Indemnity. " In Best
Film Plays, 1945. John Gassner and Dudley Nichols,
eds. New York: Crown, 1946. Reprinted, 1977,
Garland Publishing. The screenplay.

*Chastain, Thomas. "James M. Cain. " Publishers Weekly,
CCII (July 24, 1972), 40-42. Routine interview.

Childs, Marquis, and James Reston. Walter Lippmann and His Times. New York: Harcourt, Brace, & Co., 1959. Lippmann edits Cain on The World.

Cowie, Alexander. The Rise of the American Novel. New York: American Book, 1948.

Cowley, Malcolm, ed. "George Simenon." In Writers at Work. New York: The Viking Press, 1959. Interview.

Cruikshank, John. Albert Camus and the Literature of Revolt. London: Oxford University Press, 1959. (New York: Galaxy, 1960).

_____. The Novelist as Philosopher. London: Oxford University Press, 1962. On Camus.

Deming, Barbara. Running Away from Myself: A Dream Portrait of America Drawn from Films of the Forties. New York: Grossman, 1969. Distinctive insights into Double Indemnity and Postman.

*Downs, Robert B. "Southern Political Humor and Folk Lore." Southeastern Librarian, XXI (Spring, 1971), 9-21. On Cain's satirical dialogs.

Durham, Philip. Down These Mean Streets A Man Must Go: Raymond Chandler's Knight. Durham, N.C.: University of North Carolina Press, 1964.

Farber, Stephen. "Violence and the Bitch Goddess." Film Comment, X (November-December, 1974), 8-12. Extended comments on film versions of Postman, Double Indemnity, and Mildred Pierce.

*Farrell, James T. "Cain's Movietone Realism." Literature and Morality. New York: Vanguard, 1947. Argues that Cain's talent has been corrupted by movie techniques; focuses his discussion on Mildred Pierce, novel and movie.

*_____. "Do Writers Need an 'AAA'? A Debate on the Plan for American Author's Authority." Saturday Review, XXIX (November 16, 1946), 9ff. Attack on Cain's proposal for a writers' "union."

Fiedler, Leslie. Love and Death in the American Novel.

New York: Stein and Day, 1966. Page references are
to Delta paperback, 1967.

"Fifty Years of the BORZOI." Publishers Weekly, CLXXXVII
(February, 1965), 48-54.

Fowlie, Wallace. A Guide to Contemporary French Literature. New York: Meridian Books, 1957. Influence of
tough-guy novelists.

Frohock, W. M. "The Tabloid Tragedy of James M. Cain."
The Novel of Violence in America: 1920-1950. Dallas,
Tex.: Southern Methodist University Press, 1950.
Generally unsympathetic discussion of Cain's work,
emphasizing The Postman. Charges Cain with immor-
ally exploiting his raw material and manipulating his
audience. Although I quarrel with Frohock on many
points, his excellent essay is important and very interesting.

Fuller, Edmund. Man in Modern Fiction. New York: Random House, 1949, 1957, 1958. Page references to the
1958 Vintage paperback.

Gardiner, Dorothy and Katherine Sorley Walker, eds. Raymond Chandler Speaking. Boston: Houghton Mifflin,
1962.

Girard, René. "Camus' Stranger Retired." PLMA LXXIX
(December, 1964), 519-33. An unsympathetic analysis
of the narrative voice in The Stranger.

Gowans, Alan. The Unchanging Art: New Forms for the
Traditional Functions of Art in Society. Philadelphia:
J. B. Lippincott, 1971.

Gresham, Katharine. "Author Cain Doesn't Live Up to
Image." Washington Post. January 2, 1967, B1.
A routine interview that Cain resented.

Grigson, Geoffrey. The Concise Encyclopedia of Modern
World Literature. New York: Hawthorn Books, 1963.

Halliwell, Leslie. The Filmgoer's Companion. New York:
Hill and Wang, 1974. On Double Indemnity.

Haskell, Molly. From Reverence to Rape, the Treatment of

Women in the Movies. New York: Holt, Rinehart
and Winston, 1974. Discussions of Double Indemnity
and Mildred Pierce.

Haycraft, Howard, ed. The Art of the Mystery Story. New
York: The Universal Library, 1947. An excellent
collection of 48 essays. Paperback.

_____. Murder for Pleasure. New York: D. Appleton-
Century, 1941. Study of conventional detective fiction.

Hemingway, Ernest. A Farewell to Arms. New York: Scrib-
ners, 1929.

Heppenstall, Rayner. The Fourfold Tradition. Norfolk,
Conn.: New Directions, 1961. On Camus.

*Hicks, Granville. "The Hard-boiled School" (essay review
of The Magician's Wife). Saturday Review, XLVIII
(August 14, 1965), 27-28.

Hirsch, Foster. The Dark Side of the Screen: Film Noir.
San Diego: A.S. Barnes, 1981. Excellent study.
Effective use of illustrations. Extended comment on
Cain, on Double Indemnity, Postman, Mildred.

Hoffman, Frederick. The Modern Novel in America.
Chicago: Regnery, 1951, 1956.

*Hoopes, Roy. "An Appreciation of James M. Cain." New
Republic, CLXXIX (July 22, 1978), 23-6.

*_____. Cain. New York: Holt, Rinehart, and Winston, 1981.

*_____. "Hack Slays Movie Colony." American Film, VII
(October, 1981), 53-6, 84.

*_____. "Raising Cain." West Coast Review of Books,
VII, 5, (1981), 11-17.

*_____. "James M. Cain, American Novelist." The
Washingtonian (November, 1975), 186-91.

Houston, Penelope. The Contemporary Cinema. Baltimore:
Penguin, 1963.

Isaacs, Edith J.R. Theatre Arts, XX (April, 1936), 260-63.

Review of Postman as a play.

Jacobs, Lewis. The Rise of American Film. New York:
Harcourt, Brace and Co., 1939. On gangster movies.
Page references are to Teachers College Press paper-
back edition, 1968.

Jensen, Paul. "Raymond Chandler, the World You Live In."
Film Comment, X (November-December, 1974), pp. 18-
26. Extended comment on movie version of Double
Indemnity.

Kael, Pauline. Kiss Kiss Bang Bang. New York: Little,
Brown, & Company, 1968. On Postman.

_____. A review of "The Postman Always Rings Twice"
(1981 version). The New Yorker, LVII (April 6, 1981),
160-66.

Kaplan, Abraham. "The Aesthetics of the Popular Arts."
Journal of Aesthetics and Art Criticism, XXIV (Spring,
1966), 351-64.

Kazin, Alfred. On Native Grounds. New York: Harcourt,
Brace, 1942. Page references are to Anchor paperback, 1956.

Knight, Arthur. The Liveliest Art. New York: Macmillan
Co., 1957. Page references are to Mentor paperback,
1959. On Visconti's version of Postman.

Krock, Arthur. Memoirs: Sixty Years on the Firing Line.
New York: Funk & Wagnalls, 1968. Several anecdotes
about Cain on The World.

Kunitz, Stanley J. "Raymond Chandler." Twentieth Century
Authors, First Supplement. New York: H. W. Wilson
Company, 1955.

_____, ed. "James M. Cain." Twentieth Century Authors.
New York: H. W. Wilson Company, 1942.

LaValley, Albert J., ed. Mildred Pierce (Screenplay).
Madison, Wis.: University of Wisconsin Press, 1980.
Long, valuable Introduction by LaValley, "A Trouble-
some Property to Script." Notes to the screenplay,
citing variants. Faulkner worked on one of several
versions.

Lawson, John Howard. Film: The Creative Process. New York: Hill and Wang, 1964. On Double Indemnity.

*Lehan, Richard. "Camus's L'Etranger and American Neo-Realism." Books Abroad, XXXVIII (Summer, 1964), 233-38. Compares Camus' The Stranger with Cain's Postman. More detailed than A Dangerous Crossing.

_____. A Dangerous Crossing, French Literary Existentialism and the Modern Novel. Carbondale, Ill.: Southern Illinois University Press, 1973. Compares Camus' The Stranger with Cain's Postman.

*Leonard, John. "The Wish of James M. Cain." New York Times Book Review (March 2, 1969), 2, 48.

*Lerner, Max. "Cain in the Movies." Public Journal: Marginal Notes on Wartime America. New York: Viking Press, 1945. Brief but very perceptive commentary on Cain's work, on the occasion of the appearance of the movie Double Indemnity.

Levin, Harry. Contexts of Criticism. Cambridge, Mass.: Harvard University Press, 1957.

Lewis, Wyndham. The Letters of Wyndham Lewis, W. K. Rose, ed. Norfolk, Conn.: New Directions, 1963. Advises writer to learn from study of dialog in Postman and Hemingway's The Sun Also Rises.

Lottman, Herbert R. Albert Camus, A Biography. Garden City, N. Y.: Doubleday, 1979.

Luskin, John. Lippmann, Liberty, and the Press. University, Ala.: The University of Alabama Press, 1972. Quotes Cain on Lippmann and describes Cain's contribution to the World.

McCoy, Horace. They Shoot Horses, Don't They? New York: Simon & Schuster, 1935. Paperback, Avon, 1966; with screenplay, 1970. Page references are to two paperback editions.

*MacDonald, Ross. "Cain X 3" (review). New York Times Book Review (March 2, 1969), 1, 49, 51. Excellent comments on Cain's work from a tough writer of today.

MacShane, Frank. The Life of Raymond Chandler. New
     York: E. P. Dutton, 1976. Cain's relationship with
     Chandler; Chandler's comments on Cain.

Madden, David. American Dreams, American Nightmares.
     Carbondale, Ill.: Southern Illinois Press, 1968.

*_____. "Cain's The Postman Always Rings Twice and
     Camus' L'Etranger." Papers on Language and Litera-
     ture, V (Fall, 1970), 407-19.

_____. "Character as Revealed Cliché in Wright Morris's
     Fiction." Midwest Quarterly, XXII (Summer, 1981),
     319-36.

_____. Harlequin's Stick, Charlie's Cane. Bowling Green,
     Ohio: Popular Press, 1975.

*_____. James M. Cain. New York: Twayne, 1970.

*_____. "James M. Cain and the Movies of the Thirties
     and Forties." Film Heritage, II (Summer, 1967),
     9-25.

*_____. "James M. Cain and the Pure Novel." The Uni-
     versity Review--Kansas City, XXX (December, 1963),
     143-48; continued XXX (March, 1964), 235-39. A
     general discussion of Cain's novels.

*_____. "James M. Cain and the Tough Guy Novelists of
     the 30s." The Thirties. Ed. Warren French, Deland,
     Florida: Everett Edwards, Inc., 1967. Cain's novels
     in the context of other tough-guy writers.

*_____. "James M. Cain: Twenty-minute Egg of the
     Hard-boiled School." Journal of Popular Culture, I
     (Winter, 1967), 178-92. Biographical account of Cain's
     career.

*_____. "Morris' Cannibals, Cain's Serenade: The Dy-
     namics of Style and Technique." Journal of Popular
     Culture, VIII (Summer, 1974), 59-71.

_____. "The Necessity for an Aesthetics of Popular Culture."
     Journal of Popular Culture, VII (Summer, 1973) 1-14.

*_____. A Primer of the Novel. Metuchen, N.J.: Scare-

crow Press, 1980.   Essay on Postman, comments on
several other Cain novels.

_____.   Proletarian Writers of the Thirties.   Carbondale,
Ill.:   Southern Illinois University Press, 1968.

_____.   Tough Guy Writers of the Thirties.   Carbondale,
Ill.:   Southern Illinois University Press, 1968.   See
Joyce Carol Oates' essay on Cain.

_____.   Wright Morris.   New York: Twayne, 1964.

Magill, Frank N.   Masterpieces of World Philosophy.   New
York: Salem Press, 1961.

*Manvell, Roger.   New Cinema in Europe.   New York: E. P.
Dutton, 1966.   On Visconti's version of Postman.

"Massachusetts Supreme Court Clears Cain's Serenade."
Publishers Weekly, CLVIII (September 30, 1950),
1585.   Account of attempts to censor Serenade for depicting sexual depravity and desecrating religion.

Mayfield, Sara.   The Constant Circle: H. L. Mencken and
His Friends.   New York: Delacorte Press, 1968.
Cain's relationship with Mencken.

Mencken, H. L.   The American Language.   New York: Alfred A. Knopf, 1936.   Supplement One (1945).   Supplement Two (1948).

* Miller, Gabriel.   Screening the Novel: Rediscovered American Fiction in Film.   New York: Frederick Ungar,
1980.   Compares novel and MGM movie version (1946)
of Postman at length.   Also McCoy's They Shoot Horses,
Don't They? and Traven's Treasure of Sierra Madre.

Morris, Wright.   Love Among the Cannibals.   New York: Harcourt, Brace, 1957.   Paperback, Lincoln, Neb.:   University of Nebraska Press, 1977.   Same pagination as
original edition.

_____.   "Made in U. S. A."   The American Scholar, XXIX
(Autumn, 1960), 483-94.   The cliché in Morris' works.

_____.   "The Origin of a Species, 1942-1957."   Massachu-
setts Review,   VII (Winter, 1966), 121-35.   Function
of the cliché in Morris' works.

_____. The Territory Ahead. New York: Harcourt,
Brace, 1958.

Muller, Herbert J. Modern Fiction: A Study of Values.
New York: Funk & Wagnalls, 1937. Page references
are to McGraw-Hill paperback, 1964.

*Nichols, Luther. "Postman's Assistant." The New York
Times Book Review (May 13, 1962), p. 8. Interview
on the occasion of the publication of Mignon.

Nye, Russel. The Unembarrassed Muse, the Popular Arts
in America. New York: Dial Press, 1970.

*Oates, Joyce Carol. "Man Under Sentence of Death: The
Novels of James M. Cain." Tough Guy Writers of
the Thirties. Ed. David Madden. Carbondale, Ill.:
Southern Illinois University Press, 1968. Miss Oates,
author of two volumes of short stories and two novels,
exhibiting her own tough vision of sex and violence in
America, has written the best single essay on Cain's
works.

Pacifici, Sergio. A Guide to Contemporary Italian Liter-
ture. Cleveland: Meridian World, 1962. Influence of
tough-guy novelists.

Paterson, John. "A Cosmic View of the Private Eye."
Saturday Review, XXXVI (August 22, 1953), 7ff.

Place, T. A. and C. S. Peterson. "Some Visual Motifs of
Film Noir." Film Comment, X (May, 1974) 30-35.

*Postman, play The Literary Digest, CXXI (March 7, 1936),
20. Review of Postman as a play.

*Reck, Tom S. "J. M. Cain's Los Angeles Novels." Colo-
rado Quarterly, XXII (Winter, 1974), 375-87. Interesting essay; compare with Walter Wells' Tycoons and
Locusts.

Redman, Ben Ray. "Decline and Fall of the Whodunit."
Saturday Review, XXXV (May 31, 1952), 8ff.

Rexroth, Kenneth. "Disengagement: the Art of the Beat
Generation." In New World Writing, No. 11. New
York: New American Library, 1957. On Traven.

Rolo, Charles J. "Simenon and Spillane: the Metaphysics for the Millions." In New World Writing, No. 1. New York: New American Library, 1952.

Rotha, Paul. The Film Till Now. A Survey of World Cinema. New York: Twayne, 1960, rev. ed. (1949).

Schorer, Mark. Sinclair Lewis. New York: McGraw-Hill, 1961.

Schumach, Murry. The Face on the Cutting Room Floor. New York: Morrow, 1964.

See, Carolyn. "The American Dream Cheat." In Tough Guy Writers of the Thirties. Ed. David Madden. Carbondale, Ill.: Southern Illinois University Press, 1968. See also her unpublished dissertation. Tough-guy novels set in Hollywood, mostly in the thirties.

*Smith, Harrison. "The Authority." (Editorial). The Saturday Review of Literature, XXIX (September 23, 1946), 18. An attack on Cain's American Author's Authority efforts.

Smith, Thelma M. and Ward L. Miner. Transatlantic Migration: the Contemporary American Novel in France. Durham, N.C.: Duke University Press, 1955.

Snell, George. The Shapers of American Fiction. New York: E. P. Dutton, 1947.

Sontag, Susan. Against Interpretation. New York: Farrar, Straus & Giroux, 1966. Page references are to Delta paperback. See "Against Interpretation," "On Style," "Notes on Camp," and "One Culture and the New Sensibility."

Spiller, Robert E., et al. Literary History of the United States. New York: Macmillan, rev. ed., 1974.

*Starr, Kevin. "It's Chinatown." The New Republic, CLXXIII (July 26, 1975), 31-2.

Steel, Ronald. Walter Lippmann and the American Century. New York: Atlantic/Little, Brown, 1980. Many details about Cain's relationship with Lippmann on the World.

*Sturak, Thomas, "Horace McCoy's Objective Lyricism."
    In Tough Guy Writers of the Thirties. Ed. David
    Madden. Carbondale, Ill.: Southern Illinois Univer-
    sity Press, 1968. Excellent study of McCoy's fiction.
    See also Sturak's dissertation.

*Swindell, Larry. "Cain, 82, Still Writes of Faithless Sex."
    Authors in the News, Vol. 1. Chicago: Gale Research,
    1976.

*Tallack, Douglas G. "William Faulkner and the Tradition of
    Tough-Guy Fiction." In Dimensions of Detective Fiction.
    Larry N. Landrum, Pat Browne, Ray B. Browne, eds.
    Bowling Green, Ohio: Popular Press, 1976. Cain is
    the major writer with whom Faulkner is compared.
    Excellent essay.

*Thurber, James. "Hell Only Breaks Loose Once." The
    Middle-Aged Man on the Flying Trapeze. New York:
    Harper & Brothers, 1935. Parody of The Postman.

Traven, B. The Death Ship. New York: Collier Books,
    1962. (1926, 1934). Pagination cited in Chapter One
    is to this paperback edition.

Tyler, Parker. The Hollywood Hallucination. New York:
    Creative Age Press, 1944.

_____. Magic and Myth of the Movies. New York: Henry
    Holt, 1947.

Van Doren, Carl. The American Novel, 1789-1939. New
    York: Macmillan, 1921. Rev. ed., 1940.

*Van Nostrand, Albert. The Denatured Novel. Indianapolis:
    Bobbs-Merrill, 1960. Although I disagree with many
    of Van Nostrand's points, he presents an excellent
    analysis of movie elements in most of Cain's novels.

Warfel, Harry R. American Novelists of Today. New York:
    American Book Co., 1951.

Warshow, Robert. "The Gangster as Tragic Hero." "The
    Immediate Experience. New York: Doubleday & Co.,
    1964.

Weingast, David Elliot. Walter Lippmann, A Study in

Personal Journalism. New Brunswick: Rutgers University Press, 1949. Quotes Cain on Lippmann at
length.

*Wells, Walter. Tycoons and Locusts: A Regional Look at
Hollywood Fiction of the 1930s. Carbondale, Ill.: Southern Illinois University Press, 1973. Long comparison
of Postman and McCoy's They Shoot Horses, Don't
They? Claims McCoy's is the better novel.

*Wilson, Edmund. "The Boys in the Back Room: James M.
Cain and John O'Hara." New Republic, CIII (November
11, 1940), 665-66. The first serious commentary on
Cain's novels (though only The Postman and Serenade
had appeared). Reprinted with commentary on other
writers added, in Classics and Commercials. New
York: Vintage Books, 1962.

*_____. Review of Past All Dishonor. The New Yorker,
XXII (May 25, 1946), 90.

Wolfenstein, Martha and Nathan Leites. Movies: A Psychological Study. Glencoe, Ill.: Free Press, 1950.

*Zinsser, David. "James M. Cain." The Art of Fiction,
LXIX." (Interview), The Paris Review, n.v., number
73, 1978, pp. 117-38. Useful.

Zoltow, Maurice. Billy Wilder in Hollywood. New York:
G. P. Putnam's Sons, 1977. On Double Indemnity.

(For reviews of Cain's novels consult Book Review Digest;
the excepted comments offer a fascinating overview of
critical and public response to Cain's novels, from many
sources which are difficult to locate in the original.)

INDEX

Abstract, words, 80; issues, 65
Abstractions, 80
Absurd, the, 68, 81; heroes, 84; man, 84; novel, 82
Accident, 41, 55, 91
Act, from motive to, 75, 87, 91, 120
Acting areas, 99
Action, 2, 7, 12, 18, 62, 64, 69, 73, 81, 83, 122, 126; dramatic, 125; of events, 122; improvised, 99; kinetic quality of, in Cain, 125; in Morris's style, 123; novel of, 92; overt, 122; philosophical, 85
Adultery, 48, 50
Adventure, 65, 74
Adventure-mystery tale, 34
Aesthetic, 103
Aesthetic, 4, 16, 71, 93-108; concepts, 111; convictions, 42; distance, 113; emotion, 70; experience, 71, 96, 97, 106; pleasure, 3; of popular art, 97; of popular fiction, 113; principles, major, 102-106; of reaction, 107; of serious fiction, 113; stasis, 70; tradition, 96, 109
"Aesthetics of Popular Culture," 95
"Aesthetics of the Popular Arts," 106-108
Affinities, with Flaubert, 70
Against Interpretation, 95
Agee, James, 38, 50, 51, 52, 54
Agee on Film, 50, 51
Albert Camus and the Literature of Revolt, 80, 82
Alice in Wonderland, 63
Allegory, 12, 25
Allen, Hervey, 32
Allusions, 69
Allyson, June, 47
Amateur, audacious, 116; fact-armed, 73
Ambiguity, 41, 85, 107
American character, 2, 9, 37, 41, 73, 115, 116, 123
American culture, 51
American dream, x, 2, 9, 10, 13, 115, 116, 117, 123

American Dreams, American Nightmares, x
American land, 2, 9, 115, 116
American landscape, in fiction, 38
American language, 123
American literature, 61
American Magazine, The, 47
American Mercury, 8, 27, 45, 46, 73
American nightmares, 2, 9, 10, 117
American scene, 27, 34, 78
Anachronisms, 36
Anderson, Sherwood, 110
Anticipation, 91
Antinovel, 91
Appeal, to reader, 5, 73, 103; prurient, 76
Aquinas, St. Thomas, 70, 102
Arab (The Stranger), 86, 87, 88, 90
Archetypes, female, 117; mythical, 100
Architecture, 70
Arden, Eve, 52
Argot, California, 68
Aristotle, 102
Arlen, Richard, 46
Art, 29, 41, 56, 61, 65, 67, 68, 71, 78, 92, 96, 100, 103ff, 111, 120; abstract, 62; for art's sake, 110; bad, 94; cinematic, 45-46, 48; erotics of, 96; of gangster movies, 40; good, 94; highest, 103; and life not separate, 103; non-, 94; pure, 16; serious, 41, 97; what it does, 109; what it is, 109
Art as Experience, 105
Artifacts, 115
Asphalt Jungle (movie), 40
Assumptions, writers' about readers, 87, 88, 89, 108, 113, 120
Atlantic Monthly, The, 27
Atmosphere, 7, 50; of evil, 75, 76
Attitude, 2, 7, 19, 22, 83, 88; aestheric, 109, 126; ambivalent, 67; of characters in movies, 38; dispassionate, 113; neutral, 113; new 94; objective, 113; philosophical, 85; romantic, 71, 84; tough, in theater, 37

Audacity, 22, 65, 71, 73, 123;
    Byronic, 75
Auden, W. H., 3, 4
Audience, 9, 99, 100, 120
Aura, 70; of evil, 121
Auteur, 101
Authority, 122; sense of, 34
Avant-garde, 19, 98, 114
Aydelotte, William, 3

B. Traven, an Introduction, 20
Bacall, Lauren, 39
Background, 73; surreal, 68
Baltimore Sun, The, 27, 63
Balzac, 3
Barnes, Jake, 84
Barzun, Jacques, 3
Basso, Hamilton, 63
Baúmann, Michael, 20
Baxter, Warner, 47
Beautiful, the, 70, 101, 104
Beauty, 76, 98, 102, 106, 119;
    easy or difficult, 105
Becoming, process of, 118
Beery, Wallace, 39
Beethoven, 119
Beginning, of novel, 62
Bell, Clive, 97, 101
Bellow, Saul, 8, 33
Benét, William Rose, 61, 69, 113,
    122
Bennett, Bruce, 52
Bennett, Joan, 39
Best Film Plays, 48
Betrayal, 77
Bickford, Charles, 45
Big Sleep, The, 1, 38, 39; movie
    version, 38, 42
Biograph Theater, Chicago, 37
Black Mask, 4, 59
Blackmur, R. P., 40
Blees, Robert, 56
Blue Dahlia, The (movie), 38, 48
Blyth, Ann, 52, 54
Bogart, Humphrey, 39, 40
Bogdanovich, Peter, 57
Bolitho, William, 27
Bond, James, 37
Boring the reader, 126
Bosanquet, Bernard, 102, 104-105,
    109
Boyd, James, 32
Boyer, Charles, 45
"Boys in the Back Room, The," 2,
    38, 58, 61
Brackett, Charles, 48
Bravura, 73
Brazzi, Rossano, 47

Breé, Germaine, 79, 83
Breen Office, 47, 48
Brevity, 7, 18, 62, 66
Brontë, Charlotte, 111
Brown, Nacio Herb, 45
Browne, Ray, 100
Bruce, Lenny, 98
Buckler, William S., 71
Bulwer-Lytton, Edward, 108
Bunny, John, 42-43
Busch, Niven, 54, 111

Cain, James M: American Authors
    Authority, 34; American history,
    view of, 27; articles, 27; Bur-
    bank, living in, 31, 44; craft,
    78, 119, 120; craft, compared
    with subtler techniques, xi, 63;
    craft, reader's response to, xi;
    death of, 77; dialogues, 27; edi-
    tor, The Lorraine Cross, 27;
    editorial writer, 27; as entertain-
    er, 78; essays, 27, 68; Europe,
    visits, 31; fairness, sense of,
    46; fiction, significance of, x; in
    the forties, 32; health, 34; Holly-
    wood years, 31 ff; Hyattsville,
    moves to, 35; influence of his
    fiction: on fiction, xi; on Ameri-
    can fiction, 62; on European fic-
    tion, xi, 62; on movies, xi, 53;
    instructor, journalism, 27; jour-
    nalist, xi, 73; marriage, to
    Florence Macbeth, 34; on movies,
    42; New York years, 37; on per-
    iod novel, 33; plays, 31, 37, 63,
    68; popular fiction, writing as a
    career, xi; popular novelist, x,
    61, 62, 112, 113; prefaces, 63;
    reader, ideal, 120; recognition,
    62; reputation, 78, serials, 47;
    short stories, 28, 63, 68, 72;
    singer, failure as, 43; teacher,
    mathematics, 27; temperament,
    journalistic, 78; tough style, in
    nonfiction, 70; World War II, 32;
    writing, as a career, x, xi
Writings of:
    "Baby in the Icebox, The," 46
    Butterfly, The, 32, 33, 57, 61,
        62, 64, 65, 66, 68, 70, 72,
        73, 75, 78
    "Camera Obscura," 45
    Career in C Major, 7, 29, 31,
        47, 65; origin, 29
    Double Indemnity, 7, 29, 35,
        61, 72, 74, 76, 114; incep-
        tion, 29

Embezzler, The, 7, 30, 47
Facteur sonne Toujours deux
   fois, Le (Postman Always
   Rings Twice), 79
Galatea, 34, 57, 72, 75, 77
Institute, The, 35, 73
Jealous Woman, 7, 34
Love's Lovely Counterfeit,
   32, 33, 56, 68
Magician's Wife, The, 34,
   35, 68, 82, 83; reception
   of, 34; modeled on Postman, 34
Mignon, 33, 34, 73
Mildred Pierce, 7, 31, 58,
   61, 66, 68, 69, 78, 114;
   as proletarian, 31
Moth, The, 31-32, 66, 72,
   73; autobiographical elements, 31, 72; inception,
   31; as proletarian, 31
Our Government, 8, 27
Past All Dishonor, 32, 33,
   56-57, 72, 73, 77
"Pastorale," 27, 28
"Pathology of Service, The,"
   27
Postman Always Rings Twice,
   The, x, xi, 1, 6, 9-12,
   28, 29, 34, 44, 61, 62,
   64ff, 70, 76, 77, 78, 79-
   92, 93, 102, 109, 110,
   111, 113, 114; adapted to
   movies, 29; adapted to
   stage, 28, 29, 37; immoral, 67; model for Camus'
   The Stranger, 83; original
   in form, 80; lacks philosophical dimension, 91; quintessential tough-guy novel,
   1; origin of title, 28
Rainbow's End, 35, 36
Root of His Evil, The, 31,
   34, 47, 69
Serenade, xi, 6, 30, 31, 42,
   47, 56, 61, 68, 69, 72ff,
   113-126; origin, 30
Sinful Woman, 7, 32, 68
Three of a Kind, 28, 29, 69,
   126
Three of Hearts, 32, 33
"Two Can Sing" (Career in
   C Major), 30
Screenwriting: xi, 37, 43,
   44; Cain on why he failed,
   42; Algiers, 42, 45; The
   Duchess of Delmonico, 44;
   Gypsy Wildcat, 45; Hot
   Saturday, 44; Pepe Le

Moko, 45; Stand Up and
   Fight, 45; The Ten Com-
   mandments, 44
Movie Versions of Cain's Novels:
   ix, 32, 38, 57; critical recep-
   tion of, xi.
Dernier Tournant, Le (Postman
   Always Rings Twice), 56,
   79
Double Indemnity, ix, 42, 47-
   52, 53, 54, 56; influence on
   foreign films, 56
Everybody Does It (Career in
   C Major), 47
Interlude (The Root of His
   Evil, also called "The Mod-
   ern Cinderella"), 47
Mildred Pierce, ix, 49, 52-54
Ossessione (Postman Always
   Rings Twice), 56, 79
Postman Always Rings Twice,
   The, ix, 54
Serenade, 56
She Made Her Bed ("The Baby
   in the Icebox"), 46
Slightly Scarlet (Love's Lovely
   Counterfeit), 56
When Tomorrow Comes (The
   Root of His Evil), 47
Wife, Husband, Friend (Career
   in C Major), 47
Cain, James M., Mrs. (Elina Tys-
   zecka), 30
Cain, James M., Mrs. (Florence
   Macbeth), 34, 65
Cain, James William (father), 27,
   31, 64, 73
Cain, James William, Mrs.
   (mother), 30, 65
"Cain Scrutiny," 34
"Cain's Movietone Realism," 8
Cagney, James, 39
California, Southern, 2, 7, 38, 39
"Camp," 97
Camus, Albert, xi, 13, 14, 25, 42,
   61, 62, 67, 79-92, 102; Cain
   never read, 83; notebooks, 80, 83
Carrie (The Root of His Evil), 69
Carson, Jack, 52
Cause and effect, 84
Cawelti, John, 95, 96, 100, 101
Cela, Camilo Jose, 111
Céline, Louis-Ferdinand, 20
Censors, 40, 41, 48, 57
Censorship, 47, 56, 58
Challenge, 73
Chambers, Frank, 9-12, 14, 24, 55,
   66, 67, 68, 72ff, 83-92
Chance, 16, 65, 91

Chandler, Raymond, 1, 3, 4, 5, 6, 7, 16, 19, 39, 48-49, 57, 58, 111; on Cain, 6; adaptation of Double Indemnity, 48-49; on Hollywood, 45; as screenwriter, 45

"Chandler on the Film World and Television," 45

Chapter, first, 66

Character, 5, 19, 62, 64, 67, 69, 100, 101, 119

Characterization, 11, 82

Characters, 71, 73, 81, 90, 99, 113, 124, 125; Cain's, 34, 55, 61, 65, 66, 67, 68, 83; as revealed clichés, in Morris, 123; in movie, 38, 41; one-dimensional, cinematographic, 82; stereotyped, 123; in tough fiction, 7, 8, 55

Charged image, 119; in Love Among the Cannibals, 122; in Serenade, 122

Chesterton, G. K., 3

Chestertown, Maryland, 42

Christian, element, 77

Circumstance, 64, 76; force of, 41

Civil War, in Mignon, 34; in Past All Dishonor, 32

Cliché, 22, 27, 69, 73, 113, 115, 117, 118, 121, 123, 124, 125; conscious use of, 122; literary, 68; sentimental, 124; transformation of, 68

Climax, talky, 49

Cobb, Lee J., 52

Cocreators, 120

Coherence, 103, 119

Coincidence, 65, 91

Collier's, 29, 47

Collingwood, R. G., 102

Comedy, 23; low, 98

Comic, the, 65

Comic dimension, 117

Commercial elements, 78

Communication, 106

Comparative study, 110

Complexity, 67, 71, 105, 109, 111

Composition, methods of, 63

Compression, 18, 89, 122; narrative, 85

Concentration, 103

Concept, 17, 32, 64, 67, 68, 72, 74, 94, 101, 103, 104, 125; artistic, 78; defined, 119; emotive, 67; traditional, 93

"Concept of Formula in the Study of Popular Literature, The," 100

Condensation, 122

Confess, compulsion to, 71, 72

Confession, 68, 77

Conflict, 118, 124

Consciousness, events of, 122

Construction, 66

Contemporary cinema, the, 39

Content, 96, 98

Context, 94, 102, 124; psychological, 96

Contrivance, 124

Control, technical, 7, 17, 51, 68, 78, 123, 124, 125; over-control, 56

Conventions, 99, 100, 101, 108; Hollywood, 58

Cook, Elisha, Jr., 39

"Cosmic View of the Private Eye, A," 4

Costain, Thomas B., 32

Costumes, 99

Cowardice, 73; moral, 74; physical, 74

Cowboy, the, 40

Cowley, Malcolm, 62

Coxe, George, 3

Craft, 111; of popular compared with serious novel, xi

Craftsmanship, 56

Crane, Stephen, 3

Crawford, Joan, 39, 49, 52, 53, 54

Creation, a, 103

Creative energy, 62

Crenna, Richard, 52

Crime, 58, 76, 115; social, 86

Critic, 44, 46; social-minded, 42

Croce, Benedetto, 102, 103-104, 105, 106

Crofts, Freeman Will, 3

Cruickshank, John, 80, 81-82, 83, 91

Curiosity, 76

Curtiz, Michael, 52, 53

Cuteness, 69

Cynicism, 65

Dahl, Arlene, 56

Dangling Man, The, 8

Daring, 73

Darnell, Linda, 47

Dead End (play), 37

Death Ship, The, x, 9, 19-25

Debauchery, 58

"Decline and Fall of the Whodunit," 6

Dedalus, Stephan, 70

Deep Sleep, The, 114

Delusion, 68, 91

De Mille, Cecil B., 44

Deming, Barbara, 54
Dent, Lester, 3
Depression, 29, 31, 32, 40, 72
Description, 22, 69, 75, 122, 126; objective, 82, 112
Design, 120
Despair, 70
Details, 22, 72, 75, 83, 113, 115; surface, 19
Detection, novel of, formal, 3-4, 7, 8; English, 1, 3
Detective story, 37
"Detective Story as Historical Source, The," 3
Devices, fictional, 18, 45, 64, 68, 80, 85, 111, 125; confessional, 72; stock, 69
De Voto, Bernard, 3
Dewey, John, 95, 102, 105-106, 109
Dialect, 68
Dialog, x, 12, 25, 44, 48, 49, 122; climaxes, 75; effect of Cain's on scriptwriters, 58; improvised, 99; simple, 69; swiftly paced, 69
Dickens, Charles, 108
Diction, 7, 23, 68, 124; terse, 122
Dillinger, 37
Dillon, Jack (The Moth), 72, 76
Director, film, 101
Disaffiliation, 89; of tough and proletarian characters, 19
"Disengagement: The Art of the Beat Generation," 19
Doctrine, 18, 20
Doran, D.A., 43
Douglas, Paul, 47
Doyle, Arthur Conan, 63
Drama, 62, 63, 64, 73; sense of, 34
Dramatic, form, 70
Dratler, Jay, 111
Dreiser, Theodore, 3
Ducks in Thunder, 111
Duel in the Sun, 54, 111
Duke (Galatea), 75
Du Maurier, Daphne, 50, 111
Dunne, Irene, 47

Economic conditions, 24
Economy, technical, 13, 49; in prose, 80
Edification, 98
Edmunds, Walter D., 32
Effect, 5, 55, 110, 113, 119, 122; poetic, 78; terror, 125
Effort, 109

Eggar, Samantha, 52
Eilers, Sally, 46
Eliot, T. S., 3, 94
Emotion, 94, 108, 120, 125
Endings, 35, 72, 125; of Postman and The Stranger, 90
Enjoyment, 110
Entertainment, 46, 48, 78, 108, 126; aesthetics of, 108; commercial, 47; mass, 8; movies as, 43; popular, 29; pure, 2
Environment, 19, 40, 95, 106
Epical form, 70
Episodes, 64, 81
Escape, 108
Esquire, 27
Essentials, 12, 65, 82, 85, 115, 118, 123, 124
Ethical implications, 19
Evaluation, 19
Evil, aura, 71; sign of, 76
Exaggeration, on purpose, 78
Excitement, 67, 69
Execution, of effects, 122; of technique, 125
Existence, 68
Existential, 17, 21, 25, 54, 55; enlightenment, 88; literature, 67; predicament, 12, 16
Existentialism, 80, 91
Existentialist, 68, 84, 102
Experience, an, 64, 66, 70, 78, 105, 106, 126; actual, 102; aesthetic, 78, 103, 104, 108; essence of, 112; immediate, 66; itself, 107; pure, itself, 113; reader's, 12
Experiment, 80
Exploitation, of fictional elements, 8, 37
Exposition, 12, 66
Expression, 102, 103, 106; individual, 98; trite, 69
Expressionism, 78
Extremes, as method, 76
Extrinsic factors, 95

Fable, 55
Face on the Cutting Room Floor, The, 47
Facts, 73
Failure, 43
Family of Pascual Duarte, The, 111
Farewell, My Lovely (movie version: Murder, My Sweet), 38, 50
Farewell to Arms, A, 80
Farrell, Glenda, 39

Farrell, James T., 3, 8-9, 33, 41-42, 53-54, 58, 61, 66, 80
Fate, hero's, 91; tragic, 55
Faulkner, William, 12, 38, 53, 57, 70
Faults, in Cain, 36
Feeling, 103, 104, 105, 106, 108, 118, 123
Fenton, Frank, 58
Ferber, Edna, 32
Fergusson, Harvey, 44
Fiction, European, 12; nature of, 110
Fiedler, Leslie, 5, 94, 98
Field of Vision, The, 114, 123
"59 Years of the Borzoi," 28
Film noir, 42, 47, 52, 55; influence of Cain's novels on, 53
Film Till Now, The, 48
Filmgoer's Companion, The, 52
Fishwick, Marshall, 100
Fitzgerald, F. Scott, 38
Flashbacks, fictional, 81; movie, 52, 53
Flaubert, 3, 62, 70, 113
Fleming, Rhonda, 56
Focus, 69
Fontaine, Joan, 56
Food, 74, 77
For Whom the Bell Tolls, 38
Foreshadowing, 69
Forever Amber, 32
Form, 17, 63, 70, 71, 79, 99, 100, 102, 110, 116; conventional, 7; narrative, 100; pleasures of, 98
Formlessness, 107
Formula writing, 58, 61, 63, 67, 100, 101, 107, 111
Fourfold Tradition, The, 79
Foxes of Harrow, The, 110
Frame, of reference, metaphysical, 91
Freed, Arthur, 45
Freedom, 76, 100
Frenchman's Creek (movie), 50
Frohock, W.M., 9, 61, 67-68, 75, 76, 79, 83, 84-85, 91
From Here to Eternity (movie), 48
From Reverence to Rape, 54
Front Page (play), 37
Frye, Roger, 102
Fuchs, Daniel, 47
Fun, 98
Function, 109
Future, the

Gable, Clark, 37
Gales, Gerald (Death Ship), 20-25
Gamble, 65
Gangster, films, 39; as folk hero, 39, 40; as good villain, 40; sentimentalized, 40
"Gangster as Tragic Hero, The," 41
Garfield, John, 39, 55
Garrett, Richard (The Institute), 35
Gassner, John, ix, 48
Gatsby, Jay, 2
Geller, James J., 29, 47
Gide, André, 3, 62, 84
Gimmick, cinematic, 55
Glass Key, The (movie), 38
Glendale, 115
Gloria (They Shoot Horses, Don't They?), 13-18
God, 76, 77
Goff, Ivan, 56
Good Soldier, The, 120
"Good Villain and the Bad Hero, The," 40
Goodman, Philip, 37, 63
Goodness, 76
Gothic, 53
Gowans, Alan, 100, 109
Grammar, 7
Grapes of Wrath, The, 38
Graves, Robert, 3
Gravo, Rockey (They Shoot Horses, Don't They?), 14
Great Train Robbery, The, 42
Greenfield, Kent Roberts, 42
Grot, Anton de, 53
Grotesquerie, 70
Gruber, Frank, 3
Gruen, Margaret, 53
"Guilty Vicarage, The," 4
Guts, 73

Hack writers, 125
Hairy Ape, The (play), 37
Halliwell, Leslie, 52
Hamilton, Hamish, 49
Hammer, Mike, 6, 37
Hammett, Dashiell, 1, 3, 4, 5, 7, 9, 19, 38, 39, 111
Happy Death, A, 80-81
Hard-boiled, 1, 8, 16, 19, 22, 45, 82; manner, 19; picture of life, 7; private detection, novel, 1, 3, 40; private eye, 5; school, 66
Harlequin's Stick, Charlie's Cane, 100
Harlow, Jean, 39
Harmony, 70
Haskell, Molly, 54

Haycraft, Howard, 4
Heart Is a Lonely Hunter, The, 111
Heath, Percy, 43-44
Hecht, Ben, 39
Hemingway, Ernest, 3, 7, 12, 19, 27, 57, 69, 70, 73, 74, 80, 82, 87, 118
Heppenstall, Rayner, 79, 83
Hergesheimer, Joseph, 62
Hero, 35, 40, 72, 118; amateur, 116; bad, 40; Cain's typical, 73; football, 73; tough, 74; - witness, relationship, 116
Hesse, Hermann, 110
High art, 93, 95, 96, 98, 101, 110, 113; aesthetics, 106; different from popular, 101; relation to low art, 109
High culture, 94, 97; divided from low, 97
Hirshfeld, Samuel, 30
Historical accuracy, 73
Historical novels, 32, 73
History of Aesthetics, 105
Hoffmann, Frederick, 3
Holden, William, 48
Holly (Galatea), 75
Hollywood, xi, 8, 10, 13, 15, 30, 31, 37, 38, 42, 43, 44, 47, 58, 115, 116
Hollywood Hallucination, 40
Holm, Celeste, 47
Homage to Blenholt, 47
Homosexuality, 30, 74, 122
"Horace McCoy's Objective Realism," 13
Horror, 70
Houston, John, 39
Houston, Penelope, 39, 40, 49
Howell, Davy (Rainbow's End), 35
Huff, Walter (Double Indemnity; Neff in movie version), 49, 51, 72, 74
Huge Season, The, 114
Humor, 23, 65, 123; gallows, 98
Huxley, Aldous, 38
Hyman, Stanley Edgar, 9

I Should Have Stayed Home, 1
Ideas, 110
Ideology, 7
Idioms, 123
Illusion, 58, 70, 75, 107, 125; pathological, 51
Imagery, 7, 18, 38, 51, 56, 98, 103, 104, 121; American, 40
Imagination, 46, 61, 64, 94, 101, 104, 119, 120, 123, 125, 126; shaping, 119

Imitation, 70
Immediacy, 73, 84
Immediate Experience, The, 41
Impact, 94; speed of, 38
Impersonality, 70, 71, 118
Impingement, defined, 122
Implications, 125
Impressions, 66; sense, 103
Improvisation, 22, 65, 99, 123, 124; on a new life, 116
Impure, 71
In Orbit, 114
Incest, in The Butterfly, 75; in Rainbow's End, 35
Indifference, 84, 90, 117
Inessentials, 124; cliché, 115
Inevitability, 91
Inexorable, the, 91
Influences, 20; American fiction on European, xi, 2; Cain on Camus, 79-92; Cain in Europe, 115; Hemingway in France, 82; negative and positive, of movies, 45
Ingenuity, 22
Inside dope, 22, 73
Inside dopesters, 117
Instruction, 104
Intellect, 96, 118
Intellectual, 19, 104
Intelligence, 120
Intensity, 64
Intention, 63, 67, 73, 78, 91, 100, 101; philosophical, 91
Interest, 105, 110; narrative, 84
Interior monologue, 17
Interpretation, 95, 96, 119
Intricacy, 105
Intuition, 103, 104, 105, 106
Inventive powers, 119
Irony, 18, 77, 89, 90; of action, 11; minor, 12

James, Henry, 19, 63
James M. Cain, x
Jane Eyre, 111
Jazz, 41
Johnson, Nunnally, 47
Journal of Aesthetics and Art Criticism, 100, 106
Journal of Popular Culture, ix, 95, 100, 101
Journalism, 63
Joyce, James, 19, 70
Juana (Serenade), 74, 75, 77
Juxtaposition, 17, 18

K., Josef, 20
Kael, Pauline, 54-55, 56, 96

Kafka, Franz, 20, 42
Kant, Immanuel, 102
Kaplan, Abraham, 106-109
Katz (Postman Always Rings Twice), 11, 76
Kazin, Alfred, 19
Keach, Stacy, 57
Kenyon Review, The, 40
Kholmar, Fred, 43
Kinetic experience, 71
Kiss Kiss Bang Bang, 54-55
Kiss Tomorrow Goodbye, 13, 38; movie version, 38
Knight, Arthur, 56
Knopf, Alfred, 28
Knopf, Blanche, 1, 28
Know-how, 73, 117
Knowledge, character's possession of, 35; intuitive, 103
Kraft-Ebbing, 30
Krock, Arthur, 29
Krutch, Joseph Wood, 3

Ladd, Alan, 39
Ladies' Home Journal, The, 29
Lady in the Lake, The (movie), 38
Lake, Veronica, 39
Lamarr, Hedy, 45
Lange, Jessica, 55
Langer, Susanne K., 101, 102, 109
Lanza, Mario, 56
LaValley, Albert J., 52, 53
Lawrence, Vincent, 28, 37, 63, 64
Lawson, John Howard, 42
Layden, Mrs. (They Shoot Horses, Don't They?), 15, 16
Lee, Harper, 111
Lehan, Richard, 79, 83, 84, 91
Length, 7, 38, 63; in Postman and Stranger, 85; too long, 72
Lerner, Max, 49, 54, 58, 61, 65
Levin, Harry, 94
Liberty, 29, 47
Life of Raymond Chandler, The, 6-7
Limitations, external and internal, 99
Lippmann, Walter, 27, 28
Literary elements, sophisticated, 120
Literary History of the United States, 115
Literary ideals, 63
Literature and Morality, 42
Littauer, Kenneth, 47
Little Caesar (movie), 39
Liveliest Art, The, 56
Locale, simple, 86

Lockwood, Clay (The Magician's Wife), 34
Lorraine Cross, The, 27
Los Angeles, 115
Lottman, Herbert R., 80
Louisville Courier-Journal, 29
Love, 7, 74, 77; God's, 90; somatic, 76
Love Among the Cannibals, xi, 113-126
Love and Death in the American Novel, 5, 98
"Love Is Where You Find It" (song), 45
Love story, 64, 110, 120
Lovemaking, animalistic, 75
Love-rack, 10, 64, 65, 116
Lovers, the, 71; first encounters, 113
Lucienne (A Happy Death), 81
Luck, 65
Lupino, Ida, 39
Lust, 74
Lynn, Jeffrey, 47
Lyricism, 7, 65, 70; in Postman, 6

McCoy, Horace, x, 1, 2, 7, 9, 12-18, 19, 38, 39, 111; on Cain, 13
MacDonald, Jeanette, 44
MacDougall, Ranald, 52
MacMurray, Fred, 39, 48, 54
MacShane, Frank, 6-7
Madame Bovary, 50
"Made in U.S.A.," 123, 124
Madge (Postman), 11
Magic and Myth of the Movies, 51-52
Magill, Frank, 102
Malraux, Andre, 3
Maltese Falcon, The, 1, 38; movie version, 38, 41, 42, 49
Maltz, Albert, 53
Mamet, David, 55, 56
"Man Under Sentence of Death," 68
Manhattan Melodrama, 37
Mankowiecz, Tom, 57
Manvell, Roger, 56
Marie (The Stranger), 87, 90
Marlowe, Philip, 5, 6
Marshall, Brenda, 47
Marx Brothers, 41
Masculine mystique, 7
Masculinity, assumptions about, 88
Mason, Van Wyck, 32
Mass culture, 123
Mass media, 99, 124; reportage, 72
Masses, the, 19
Masterpieces of World Philosophy, 102

Maugham, Somerset, 3, 110
Meaning, 61, 64, 67, 70, 96, 119
Medium, 105; itself, 110
Melodrama, 41, 48, 49, 53, 54, 65
Memory, 105
Mencken, H. L. , 8, 63
Mersault, Patrice, (A Happy Death), 80-81
Metalious, Grace, 110
Metaphor, 23, 24, 54; marathon dance as existential, 21; ship as existential, 21, 25
Method, Camus's, 82
Metro Goldwyn Mayer, 44, 48, 54, 56
Meursault, 14, 17, 24, 61, 67, 68, 72, 83-92
Mexico, 47, 115, 116, 119
Midwestern speech, 123
Mildred Pierce (film script, published), 52-53
Milieu, criminal, 4; gangster and private eye, 73
Miller, Gabriel, 55
Miller, Henry, 20
Milne, A. A. , 3
Mintz, Sam, 44
Mitchell, Margaret, 32
Modern Fiction, 19
Modern Novel in America, The, 3
Moments, dramatic, 122; of perception, in Morris, 126
Money, 8, 10, 35, 50, 51, 52, 71, 74ff, 81
Montez, Maria, 45
Moral, elements, 18, 40, 48, 52, 62, 65, 66, 71, 75, 87, 98, 104; significance, 67; the study of popular culture for, 94; value, 96
Moralizing, Hollywood, 49
Moran, 31
More, Paul Elmer, 3
Morgan, Frank (To Have and Have Not), 87
Morris, Chester, 39
Morris, William, agency, 47
Morris, Wright, ix, x, xi, 33, 69, 111-126; and his readers, 120
Motifs, 17, 64; animal, 96; complex pattern of, 69; complexity of, 89
Motive, 69, 75, 83, 84, 87, 91; for confessing, 72; evolution of, 72; religious, 71; social purpose, 72
Movement, 64
Moviegoers, 40, 100
Movies, 2; adaptations of fiction to, xi; effect of novels on movies, 38; effect on novels, 38; effect, negative, on Cain's novels, 38, 57; gangster, 40, 41; gangster cycle of, 39; tough, 39, 41; writing for, xi, 43, 45
Muller, Herbert J. , 19
Muni, Paul, 39
Murder, 7, 8, 9, 10, 11, 18, 28, 30, 35, 50, 52, 54, 64, 74, 75, 77, 85, 87
Murder for Pleasure, 4
Music, 30, 62, 64, 70; in Cain's novels, 65
Mussolini, 79
My Uncle Dudley, 122
Mysteries, murder, 53, 67
Mystical reunion, 77
Mystique, love, 76; lovers, 71; religious, 75
Myth, 27
Mythic land, 123; terms, 16

Napoleon, 28
Narration, retrospective, 84
Narrative, 52, 62, 63, 64, 83, 125; skill, 12; technique, 37; tepidity, 125; thrust, 89
Narrator, 23, 85, 112, 113; tells, 72; writes, 72
Nathanael West: The Cheaters and the Cheated, x
Nation, The, 27
Natural, a, 65, 82
Naturalism, 19; European, 1
Neilson, James M. , 30
Neorealism, American, 79
New Cinema in Europe, 56
New Letters, ix
New Republic, The, 2
New York, 116
New York World, The, 27
New Yorker, The, 27, 56, 57
Newsweek, 34
Nichols, Luther, 33
Nicholson, Jack, 55
Nietzsche, 102
Nirdlinger, Phyllis (Double Indemnity), 49, 51, 74
No Pockets in a Shroud, 13
Norris, Frank, 3
Nostalgia, 93, 95, 96, 98, 114
"Notes on 'Camp,'" 97
"Notes Toward an Aesthetic of Popular Culture," 101
Notion, defined, 119
Novel, of action, 87; of character, 92; of self-knowledge, 87

Novel of Violence in America, The, 67, 79ff
Novelist as Philosopher, The, 80
Novelists, American, 82
Novels in the Making, 71
Nye, Russel, 95, 99

Oates, Joyce Carol, 68
Object, 102; in itself, 105; mass-produced, 98
Objectification, 106
Objective, view of characters, 12
Objective writer, 81
Objectivity, impersonal, 119
O'Brien, Pat, 39
Obscenity, 75
O'Connell, Father (The Postman), 90
O'Hara, John, 2, 3, 19, 57
Omission, skillful, 122
On Native Grounds, 19
"One Culture and the New Sensibility," 97
Open road, the, 84
Openings, of novels, 125
Opera, 30, 34, 43, 65; singer: Cain, 65; hard-boiled, 73; mother, 30, 65; wife, 65
Optimism, tough, 65
Organization, technical, 65
"Origin of a Species," 123
"Oscar Night in Hollywood," 45
Outsider, the, 83, 72
Outsider, The (The Stranger), 79
Overtones, melancholy, 123; religious, 91

Pace, xi, 7, 12, 13, 49, 55, 56, 58, 62, 64, 69, 75, 85, 125, 126; cinematic, 69; in movies, 38; in stage drama, 38; theatrical, 69
Pagan, element, 77
Painting, nonobjective, 70
Palmer, Lloyd (The Institute), 35
Papadakis, Cora, (Postman), 10-12, 66, 67, 68, 69, 72, 75, 76, 77, 83, 84, 86, 88, 89, 90
Papadakis, Nick (Postman), 10, 11, 66, 67, 72, 75, 89
Parallels, 90, 92, 121-122
Paramount studios, 43
Paris Review, 63, 83
Passion, 64, 65, 77
Past, the, 32, 83, 118, 126; dead, 123
Paterson, John, 4-5

Patterns, 12, 18, 64, 66, 71, 91, 101, 123; narrative, 72; thematic, 72, 116
Payne, John, 56
Pearson, Norman Holmes, ix
Perception, original meaning of "aesthetic," 101; psychology of, 96
Perelman, S. J., 98
Petrified Forest, The (play), 37
Peyton Place, 110
Phantom Circuit, of imagination, 46
Phenomenologists, 102
Philosophical element, 13, 62, 63, 104; concept, 92; novel, 81; passages, 81; relevance, 83; view, 67
Phony, 124
Physical drives, 19
Picaresque, 23; novel, 72
Pierce, Mildred, 31, 52, 53, 69, 75
Pierce, Veda, 52, 69
Pierson, Louise, 53
Plains Song, 114
Plastic arts, 70
Plato, 102
Pleasure, 102, 106; aesthetic, 109; aesthetic, pure, 101
Plot, 5, 23, 41, 58, 101, 113, 119, 125; absence of, 85; complex, 86; construction, 82
Poe, Edgar Allan, 3, 7, 63
Poem, 66
Poet, Cain as, 61, 126
Poetry, 123
Point of view, explicit or implicit, 91
Point of view, first person, 7, 52, 68, 72, 85; third person, 68; third person, omniscient, 68
Political elements, 110; conditions, 24; values, 96
Popular and serious fiction, differences, 109-126
Popular art, 93-108, 110; self-centered, 108
Popular artist, 99
Popular culture, 93-108, 114; affinities with avant-garde, 98; forces that produce, 95; understanding, ix, 37
Popular culture aesthetics, xi, 93-109, 126
Popular elements, 78, 120
Popular fiction, 2, 24, 113
Popular mind, values of, 95
Popular novels, 111, 120
Possibilities, 124
"Postman's Assistant," 33

Powell, Dawn, 9, 125
Powell, Dick, 39
Powell, William, 39
Power, 28, 71
Powers, Tom, 48
Predicament, 12, 90, 92
Present, 83, 84, 117, 118, 123,
    126; historical, 84; phony, 115,
    116
Pride, 74
Pride and Prejudice, 110
Priest, in The Stranger, 90
Process, over raw material, 122
Progeny, mystery of, 76
Proletarian, the, 5, 83
Proletarian fiction, x, 1, 19, 37,
    56; Death Ship, example of, 19-
    25; disinherited in, 89; Mildred
    Pierce, as, 31; The Moth, as,
    31; sagas, 119; compared with
    tough fiction, 9; influence on
    tough fiction, 19; violence in, 19
Proletarian writers, x, 13, 19, 25,
    53, 115
Proletarian Writers of the Thirties,
    x
Psychology, 95, 96, 110; of char-
    acters, 12, 51, 52; Gestalt, 96;
    of reading, 96
Public Journal, 49
Pure novel, xi, 62, 65, 66, 68,
    70, 71, 78, 91, 113
Purification, 71
Purity, 77

Radiance, 70
Rafelson, Bob, 55, 56
Raft, George, 39
Raphaelson, Samson, 30
Raw material, 17, 27, 119, 122;
    simple, 74
Raymond (The Stranger), 86, 88
Raymond Chandler Speaking, 119
Razor's Edge, The, 110
Reaction, 108
Reader, the, 24, 25, 39, 58, 64,
    73, 83, 87, 89, 91, 113, 120,
    126; as accomplice, 67; author
    relationship, 120; boring, 64;
    Cain and, 8-9, 10, 46, 67; cap-
    tive, 66; community of, 120; in-
    volve, intimately, 73; moral
    attitudes of, 88; mind of, 119;
    receptive, 119; response, mani-
    pulation of, 11; serious, 11, 70,
    78
Real thing, 118, 123, 124
Realism, 5, 53, 55, 78, 82, 100;

Hollywoodized, 53; movietone,
    41-42, 58, 61; Objective, 19;
    postwar, Italian, 56; pseudo-, 41;
    psychological, 19, 53; selective,
    19; selective American, 1; seri-
    ous, 41
Reality, 105
Rebecca, 111
Rebel, The, 82
Rebirth, 71
Receptivity, 109
Recognition, 107
Record, the, 73
Red Harvest, 3-4
Redbook, 29
Redemption, 71, 77, 86
Redman, Ben Ray, 6
Religion, 74, 77, 90, 91; pagan
    Christian, 71
Research, 34, 73
Response, 105; aesthetic, 108
Responsibility, 73, 90
Reviewers, 32, 40
Revision (drafts), 33, 83
Rexroth, Kenneth, 19, 94
Rhetoric, 19, 23, 104
Rhythm, 62, 64, 123
Risk, 65
Riskin, Robert, 58
Ritual, 77, 101; purification, 77
Robbe-Grillet, Alain, 19
Robert (They Shoot Horses, Don't
    They?), 13-18
Roberts, Ben, 56
Robinson, Edward G., 39, 48
Rodin, 63, 64
Romance, conventional, 71
Romantic, 6, 74, 81
Romanticism, 25, 40, 74; American,
    masculine, 65
Rotha, Paul, 45, 48
Running Away From Myself, 54
Ruskin, Harry, 54

Sackett (Postman), 11, 89
Sacrilege, 76
Sale, Richard, 3
Santayana, George, 95, 102, 105,
    106
Saroyan, William, 2
Sartre, Jean Paul, 79
Satire, 65
Saturday Evening Post, The, 27
Sayers, Dorothy, 3
Scarface (movie), 39
Scene, 12, 64, 86, 116, 125; death
    cell, 90; Mexican, 117; sex, 54
Schizophrenia, of those who study

popular culture, 93, 94; aesthetic, 94
Schopenhauer, 102
Schulberg, Budd, 38
Schumach, Murry, 47, 48
Screening the Novel, 55
Scott, Zachary, 52
Sculpture, Greek, 64, 70
Secret Confessions, 100
Selectivity, 122
Self-deception, dialectics of, 66
Self-dramatization, 73, 117; American compulsion to, 27
Self-knowledge, 91
Sense of Beauty, The, 102
Sensibility, new, 94, 97, 98; active, 126
Sensory experience, 96
Sentimentality, 6, 40, 58, 65, 87, 90, 108, 119
Serious elements, 78, 120, 126
Serious fiction, 111, 113; aesthetics of, 126
Serious writers, 2, 112, 113
Setting, 7, 39, 101; bizarre, 75; symbolic, 15
Sex, 8, 12, 15, 50, 51, 52, 54, 58, 61, 71, 73, 75, 76, 87, 88, 90, 117, 118; abnormal, 75; cannibal, 121; homicidal, 54; aura of unnatural, 75; reality, 117
Sharp, John (Jack) Howard (Serenade), 42, 72, 73, 74, 75, 77
Short stories, formula, 111; serious, 111
Show, 126
Siddhartha, 110
Significance, 40, 41, 50, 77
Simenon, Georges, 62, 63, 66
Simple Art of Murder, The, 4, 5-6
Simpleton, the, 82
Simplicity, 7, 108, 109; impression of, 67
Simultaneity, 18
Sistrom, Joseph, 48, 49
Sisyphus, 16, 18, 25
Situations, 8, 66, 67, 69, 71, 85, 119, 125
Skill, 99, 101; technical, 99
Slang, 123
Snobbery, 98
Soap Opera, 41
Social, elements, 41, 53, 95, 98, 110, 111; functions of art, 109; awareness, 72; conditions, 24, 119; consciousness, 34; evils,

5, 9; responsibility, 72; significance, 8, 115; values, 2, 62, 66, 96
Society, picture of, 115; on trial, 88
Socks (They Shoot Horses, Don't They?), 15
Sontag, Susan, 96, 97-98
Space, 63
Spade, Sam, 5, 40
Speech, pattern of, 68
Spell, Cain casts, 120
Spillane, Mickey, 6
Spiller, Robert E., 115
Spirit of the times, 39, 115
Stanislav (The Death Ship), 22, 23
Stanwyck, Barbara, 39, 48, 50, 54
Statistics, use of in studying popular culture, 95
Steinbeck, John, 2, 80
Sterility, 123
Stimuli, 83, 104
Stock expectations and responses, reversal of, 120
Storm, Hans Otto, 2
Story, as story, 62, 72; manipulation of, 125
Story line, 23
Strange Love of Martha Ivers, The, 50
Stranger, The, xi, 12, 79-92, 100, 102, 111; genesis of, 83; opposite of pure novel, 91
Stripping process, 121; materially and spiritually, 118
Structure, 18, 85; episodic, 52; narrative, 100; symbolic, 91; technical, 12
Student, the, 110
Sturak, Thomas, 13, 15, 16
Style, xi, 12, 19, 20, 23, 36, 39, 53, 61, 62, 64, 68, 69, 71, 72, 79, 96, 97, 98, 101, 119, 125, 126; active, 122; Cain's, 122; Camus', 82; no comment, 85; dictates of, 123; expressionistic, 53; of A Happy Death, 81; of hard-boiled writers, 80; Hemingway's credo, 80; Morris's, 123; similar in Postman and Stranger, 85; tough, 68
Stylist, Morris as, 122
Stylization, 82
Subject, 63, 82; special, 73
Subject matter, 70
Subjectivism, romantic, 19
Suggestion, 122
Superfluity, 118
Superstition, 76

Surfaces, hard, 54
Suspense, 74
Swanson, H. N. , 57
Symbolic action, 16, 120
Symbols, 69, 82, 110, 120, 121, 123; Horter's car, 121; for character flaws, 121; of evil, 76; marathon dance, 16; in Moth, 74; natural, 13; organic relation to entire novel, 121; many readers resent, 120
Sympathy, for main characters, 64
Syntax, 7

Tale, anecdotal, 23
Taste, 56, 95ff, 102, 107, 113, 121; popular, 41; public, 53
Taylor, Robert, 45
Teacher, the, 110
Teaching, popular fiction, 110
Technique, 61, 63, 64, 65, 67, 71, 72, 82, 85, 110, 119, 125; basic, 111; cinematic, 3; expressionistic, 53; degeneration of, 6; fictional, xi, 5; hardboiled, 6; Morris's use of, 120; pure, 71; of scriptwriting, 43, 45; virtuosity in, 42
Television, 52
Tell, 126
Telling, the, 23, 24
Temptation, 19
Ten Commandments, The, 44
Tense, shifts, 84
Tension, 6, 49, 50, 67, 85, 99, 105; dramatic, 37; phony, 61; rhetorical, 122
Territory Ahead, The, 123
Terror, 64, 70, 119; effect, 125
Theater, 37
Theatergoer, 100
Theme, 24, 28, 56, 67, 68, 71, 110, 113, 115, 117, 118, 119, 125; love and death, 65; mongering, 120; in movies, 38; serious, 72 They Shoot Horses, Don't They? x, 1, 9, 12-18, 38; movie version, 38
They Won't Believe Me (movie), 51
Thin Man, The (movie), 38
Three Lectures on Aesthetics, 104
Thriller, the, private eye, 7
Time, 64, 116; span, 86
Time, 120
TLS, 15
To Kill A Mockingbird, 110-111
Tolstoy, 102-103, 105, 106
Tone, 2, 7, 27, 36, 53, 81, 123; in movies, 38; southern, 68

Tough guy, 40, 48; mystique, 27; school, 31
Tough-guy novel, 1-9, 12, 20, 22, 24, 32, 41, 79, 80, 92, 115; American, 82; American, reception in France, 79; compared with proletarian, 9; definition, 58-59; effect of movies on, 38; effect on movies, 38; influence, 81; literary descent of, 3; pure, x, 1, 7, 12; school, 13, 62; as social document, 2
Tough-guy writers, 18, 35, 77; influence in Europe, 115
Tough Guy Writers of the Thirties, x
Townsend, Dr. , 30
Tracy, Spencer, 39
Tragedy, 41, 49, 58, 63, 64
Tragic stature, 67
Transcendence, 103, 108
Transfiguration, 103
Transformation, 92, 96, 108, 116, 119, 124, 125
Transitions, 23, 66; sudden narrative, 86
Transmutation, of the mediocre, 99
Transparence, 96
Traven, B. , x, 1, 9, 19-25, 38
Treasure of Sierra Madre, The, 23, 38
Trial, The, 20
"Tribute to a Hero, " 73
Trickery, author's, 75
True Confessions, 115
Turney, Catherine, 53
Turner, Lana, 39, 55
Twentieth Century Authors, 5, 122
Twist, John, 56
Tyler, Jess (The Butterfly), 75
Tyler, Parker, 40, 41, 51, 54
Types, 110

Ugly, the, 104
Unchanging Art, The, 109
Unconscious, the, 53
Understanding, 108; process of, 116
Understatement, technique of, 85
Underworld (movie), 39
Unembarrassed Muse, The, 95, 99
Unity, 66, 103
Universals, 103
Urgency, 69
Useful, the, 104

Valery, 62
Vanity Fair, 27
Victims, 24

Villains, 47
Violence, x, 2, 3, 5, 8, 10, 12, 27, 37, 39, 52, 61, 67, 73, 74, 75, 76, 77, 84, 85, 116, 117; animal, 87; death, 66; of left-wing writing, 19; serious novel of, 67; sexual, 11; social communion with, 72
Visconti, Luchino, 56, 79
Vision, 20, 27, 55, 62, 95, 119; absurd, 91; community of, 116; creative, 78; double in popular culture studies, 109; of life, 78, 125; pure, 19; subjective, 119; tough, 7, 9
Voice, aggressive, 117
Von Sternberg, Josef, 39

Wagner, Robert, 57
Waiting for Lefty (play), 37
Wald, Jerry, 52, 53
Warner Brothers, 31, 52, 53
Warren, Robert Penn, 33, 110
Warshow, Robert, 41
Washington College, 27, 73
Waugh, Evelyn, 38
Weidman, Jerome, 19
Welleck, René, 94
Welles, Orson, 57
West, Nathanael, x, 2, 98
West Virginia Mountains, 57, in The Butterfly, 32
What Is Art? 102
Whatness, pure, 110
Whitfield, Raoul, 3

Whitman, Walt, 11, 74
Wholeness, 70
Wilder, Billy, 48-49, 50
Wilson (movie), 49
Wilson, Edmund, 2, 13, 38, 54, 57, 58, 61, 72, 115, 126
Wilson, Woodrow, 49
Winesburg, Ohio, 110
Winterset (play), 37
Winsor, Kathleen, 32
Wisdom of the body, 116, 117
Wish, that comes true, 10, 11, 12, 35, 54, 64, 68, 73, 74, 75, 114, 117
Wit, 23, 65, 98
Witness, 72, 116, 118
Wolf, Leonard, ix
Wolfert, Ira, 33
Women, Cain's, 74
Woollcott, Alexander, 27
Work, in The Death Ship, 21, 22; gospel of, 25; mystique, 25
Works of Love, The, 114
World Enough and Time, 110
Writers at Work, 62, 63

Yerby, Frank, 110
Yordan, Philip, 58
Yorikke, The, 21-25
Young, Loretta, 47
Young, Robert, 51

Zagreus (A Happy Death), 81
Zola, 3, 18